Healing Prayer

Workbook 5

of the series,
Living a Supernatural Life Naturally

A Path to Emotional and Spiritual Health
for Yourself and Others

by Linda Morgan

Healing Prayer
Workbook 5
of the series,
Living a Supernatural Life Naturally
by Linda Morgan

Healing Prayer
by Linda Morgan
Part Five of the series, *Living a Supernatural Life Naturally*

ISBN 978-1-954509-10-8

Cover photo credit: istockphoto.com/loeskieboom

Printed in the United States
visionrun.com

Vision Run Publishing

About the Author

Linda Morgan

Linda Morgan is a wife, mother, grandmother, business owner, and gifted Christian teacher. She is well known for her ability to express spiritual principles in everyday language. After being introduced to the person of the Holy Spirit in the 1970s, she has spent the years since then studying and sharing what she's learned with others.

She has ministered and taught in churches in the U.S., at retreats, through keynote addresses, and on mission trips to Europe and Central America. Linda has also had a personal prayer ministry for hurting people for over thirty years. She is passionate about helping others resolve inner and outer conflict through prayers that heal the heart and change lives.

As a business owner, she also consults and speaks to individuals and professionals alike on the importance of first impressions, and works with clients on wardrobe, color, style, and makeup.

Linda and her husband Dell make their home in Knoxville, Tennessee. They have been married since 1972 and have two grown children and seven grandchildren.

Dedication

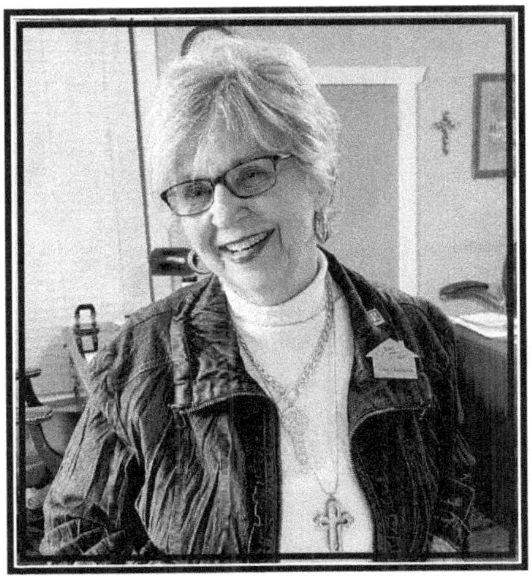

This workbook is lovingly dedicated to the memory of my dear friend Joan Champion.

Joan, true to your name, you were my biggest champion and your insight and encouragement kept me grounded in so many ways. You will be missed by so many whose lives you touched. You were such an expression of God's love to everyone you met and you truly loved God with all your heart, soul, and strength.

Contents

Living a Supernatural Life Naturally: Course Overview

Workbook 1:

- **Grace** is not just God's favor; it is also His empowerment to us so that we can overcome our weakness and sin to do His will (Romans 6:14). Everyone who has grace has the Holy Spirit living in them and can live a supernatural life naturally. Jesus wants to live His life through us, as us.
- **The Gift** of the Holy Spirit was sent to us as a Helper. The Holy Spirit is a Person, not just an impersonal influence. Jesus did not leave us helpless (John 14:26, 15:26). Being filled with the Spirit is continual (Ephesians 5:18). Spiritual gifts are supernatural manifestations of God's power provided by the Holy Spirit.
- **Living a Life of Faith** is like a mustard seed that must be planted, watered, fertilized, protected, and pruned. True spiritual life flows from our spirit and affects our mind. Faith is a gift of grace. Faith is taking that first step without seeing what is ahead. Faith occurs when we stop trying to do something by our own efforts and trust the Lord to do it for us. Belief and faith are not the same. Acting on our belief means we have faith.

Workbook 2:

- **The Power of Prayer** happens when we believe that God is and that He rewards those who seek Him. Answered prayer affirms us (Hebrews 11:6). We pray because we believe (have faith) and hope that prayer changes things. Prayer is not overcoming God's reluctance but embracing His willingness.
- **Listening Prayer** is when the Holy Spirit leads and guides us into all truth, although we have to develop a listening ear (John 16:13). God speaks to us both indirectly and directly; He is always speaking, but we are not always listening. God speaks to us and through us (1 Corinthians 12).

- **Obedience** Isaiah 1:19 says if we are willing and obedient, we will eat the good of the land. Obedience brings revelation (John 14:6). It is a key to destiny, which comes faster when we are obedient. Grace empowers us to live a life of obedience, and it empowers us to live beyond our abilities (John 21:15-17).

Living in the age of the New Testament means we are covered by grace and are under a new covenant. A covenant that means we don't have to work and struggle because we can rest in what Christ has provided. *We have the gift of the Holy Spirit, the very presence of Jesus living in us and enabling us to live a supernatural life, naturally.* It requires trusting that He is doing just that, and we don't have to make things happen. We pray, listen, and obey what the Spirit is saying. If we make a mistake and miss it (and sometimes we will), we confess, repent, and ask Him to empower us to do better. He has delegated spiritual authority to us, and when our hearts are right and our motives are pure, we can be effective over the enemy.

Workbook Three: Spiritual Authority

To defeat the enemy, we must realize and believe we have been delegated authority in the spirit realm. The blood of Jesus and His resurrection defeats the enemy once and for all. We operate from a place of victory because He has already won and delegated His authority to believers. We have been given authority in the spirit realm, which enables us to win our battles in the natural realm too. This is how we live supernaturally, naturally.

Workbook Four: Spiritual Warfare

Spiritual warfare can sound violent or challenging, but it's actually neither. It's simply recognizing the enemy and defeating him through prayer, while using the Sword of the Spirit — the Word of God — against him. We do need to understand Satan's strategy in order to know how to defeat him. To do that, we must realize and believe we have been given authority in the spirit realm. We are more than conquerors (Romans 8:37; 1 John 4:4)!

Workbook Five: Healing Prayer

We often think of healing prayer as one of the 1 Corinthians 12 gifts for healing the body given by the Holy Spirit. But healing prayer as we're discussing it, is about healing the heart. Any Christian can use this workbook, either individually or in partnership with a few others, to allow the Spirit to touch and begin to heal deeply wounded places in our hearts. It's a powerful tool to help find victory and healing to experience a more vibrant walk. In short, it's a path to emotional and spiritual healing.

Workbook Six: Destiny and Inheritance

It's hard to live in your destiny according to God's plan for your life and leave a legacy if you don't know who God created you to be. *Destiny and Inheritance* is a workbook about agreeing with God and discovering His path for you. Once you know God's plan for your life, the next challenge involves overcoming the obstacles in the way of living it out. It requires learning to rest in the assurance that God has a special design for your life, a unique destiny and inheritance beyond anything you could have imagined.

How to Use This Workbook

This workbook is the fifth in a series, *Living a Supernatural Life Naturally*. While the workbooks have been designed to be used in sequence, they can also stand alone, and this one is no exception. Whether you are experienced in healing prayer or just hearing of it for the first time, this workbook should be helpful to you. The prior workbooks in the series will be good resources for further study as well, but they are not essential to get good value from this one right now.

The first section, Learning About Healing Prayer, is a teaching on what healing prayer is and what it is based on. This section has information not covered elsewhere and also pulls on previous workbook topics to demonstrate the biblical basis for healing prayer; it delves into the principles behind each step in the process. This is a Bible study *about* healing prayer with discussion questions, journaling opportunities, assignments, and personal prayers that are familiar in format if you've used the previous workbooks in the series.

The second section, Action Steps to Healing Prayer for Yourself and Others, contains the specific steps involved in healing prayer. After learning about healing prayer in the first section, you now have the background necessary to start your journey of healing. This section has all the instructions for *conducting* healing prayer. I'd strongly recommend that you go through the process first yourself by yourself or with one or two trusted friends. After that, you'll be ready to lead others who need ministry through the process.

Between the two main sections, you'll find a number of personal testimonies from those who have gone through the healing prayer process and found it extremely helpful. As you'll see, each experience is different. We serve a God who meets us exactly where we are and supplies all our needs.

Finally, there are plenty of additional resources in the Appendix.

Section One

LEARNING ABOUT HEALING PRAYER

The Spirit of the Lord God is upon me, because the Lord has anointed me to bring good news to the poor; he has sent me to bind up the brokenhearted, to proclaim liberty to the captives, and the opening of the prison to those who are bound; to proclaim the year of the Lord's favor, and the day of vengeance of our God; to comfort all who mourn; to grant to those who mourn in Zion—to give them a beautiful headdress instead of ashes, the oil of gladness instead of mourning, the garment of praise instead of a faint spirit; that they may be called oaks of righteousness, the planting of the Lord, that he may be glorified. They shall build up the ancient ruins; they shall raise up the former devastations; they shall repair the ruined cities, the devastations of many generations.

Isaiah 61:1-4 (ESV)

Lesson 1: Healing Prayer

Healing prayer is a path to emotional and spiritual health for yourself and others. As such, it is a valuable tool to learn on your journey to ever-increasing spiritual maturity and Christ-likeness. This can be an important step toward fully experiencing your destiny in God.

There are many examples of healing and deliverance prayers throughout the Bible. In fact, healing and deliverance were the focus of the disciples' first assignment, as Jesus sent them out to minister to and evangelize the countryside **(Mark 6:7, Luke 9:1-3, 6 ESV)**.

We're going to be covering His promises in the area of healing and working on deepening your relationship with all three persons of the Godhead: Father, Son, and Holy Spirit. We want to learn to listen, trust in God's promises, stand in our delegated authority, and be as free and healthy as we can be as we grow in Christ. In healing prayer we pray through the Father, the Holy Spirit leads, and Jesus speaks truth, bringing freedom **(Ephesians 2:18)**.

In the previous study, *Spiritual Warfare* (Workbook 4), we learned that there is a very real spiritual world outside of our physical realm and view, and it's not all good. These powerful forces are at war, and the battlefield is in our minds, lives, hearts, and circumstances. In Workbook 3, *Spiritual Authority*, we learned that God has prepared us for that battle through the delegated authority we have in Christ. Together, these studies and concepts comprise a helpful foundation for moving on to healing prayer. As believers, our spirits have been sealed with the Holy Spirit and are eternal. But our bodies, minds, and emotions are still living in a fallen world, which is ruled and influenced by the "spiritual forces of evil" (Ephesians 6:12). Healing prayer is one of the ways we do battle in the spiritual realm, following the examples given to us in scripture.

A normal part of the Christian walk.

God is never done with us; we are constantly being transformed into His image. So it is no mystery that healing prayer rarely happens in just one session. Somewhat like peeling the proverbial onion, you'll often find more to work through as the first issues get cleared away. This is normal and designed to be a natural part of our supernatural walk with Jesus.

Remember that healing prayers are prayers that transform our mind, will, and emotions, which can then affect our body.

My prayer for you is that after completing the lessons in this book you will have:

- Learned to better listen to and recognize the voice of God.
- Reached a deeper level of intimacy with the Lord that will spill over into your relationship with others.
- Experienced freedom from things that are stumbling blocks in your path preventing you from walking fully in the gifts and calling of God.
- Recognized any wrong thinking you've been enslaved by, recognized and identified any lies you've believed and come to an understanding about how they affect you today.
- Will have begun to look to God for help first instead of

other more popular or worldly places[1].

- Seen that healing prayer can help when you're hindered by your past, and experience what a powerful tool it is to be able to exercise your authority in Christ through the Holy Spirit to unhinder both your present and your future.
- An experiential knowledge that when Jesus sets you free, you will really be free (John 8:36).

1 Healing prayer works in a complimentary fashion with counseling, addressing spiritual elements that counseling alone doesn't typically access.

Freedom through hearing God.

Through healing prayer, we can bring to light the places sin, either our own or others, has caused a stronghold. Our wounded hearts are healed when we allow Jesus to speak truth that brings freedom. Jesus is full of truth and grace (John 1:14), so allowing Him to speak truth to those places where we need healing brings freedom.

God talks about our needs when He says, *The Lord is near to the brokenhearted and saves the crushed in spirit* (Psalm 34:18 ESV). Again in Proverbs 17:22 and 25:28, you can see He knows what is good for us and what does us harm, whether or not it crosses the line into sin. Moreover, He expects us to do our part to pursue Him and choose what is good and fruitful.

Sometimes there are wounds from our past, either before or after we were saved, that result in faulty thinking. Deep wounds can come from trauma, cultural influence, or our own faulty thinking due to ignorance of what the Word says. We can be wounded from false teaching, guilt, insecurity, legalism, etc., because we still live in a fallen world. That's why healing prayer is such a necessary part of our supernatural walk with Christ — it helps us claim and keep the freedom He came to provide.

Hopefully by the end of this study, we will have learned how to abide in Him as He commanded (John 15:3-5).

According to John 8:34-36, we are enslaved to sin when we allow our past to dictate our future and paralyze our present life in certain areas. Jesus wants to lead us to truth so we really are free indeed from our past mistakes. This freedom means we not only stop repeating our past, but we also no longer identify with it. Instead, we are confident in our new identity in Christ. We no longer carry the burdens of guilt, shame, and regret into our present or our future. For example, see how Jesus ministered inner healing to Peter in John 21:17-19. Peter need healing from the guilt and shame of believing the lie that Jesus could not use him as a result of his sin of denying Christ. When Jesus spoke to him, it released him into his destiny.

Listening for God's voice.

The key to experiencing this kind of freedom and growth in Christ is hearing the voice of God. He sometimes speaks in a general way, and other times He is very specific. It's important to hear God and practice listening to His voice. You may hear a whisper, see a picture of something, or have thoughts come to mind. If it's edifying and brings peace, go with it and trust He is speaking to you.

When are you at your best? Whether it's morning, evening, or afternoon, meet with Him then.

Preparing to hear the Lord speak:

- Be deliberate with a time and place and make an appointment with God.
- Worship helps create an atmosphere that invites the

presence of God. Be still, quiet your mind, and worship. Enjoy the silence, or if you prefer, play Christian music that helps usher you into His presence.

- Focus in your mind's eye on a picture of Jesus or sense His presence.
- Tune in to the spontaneity of flowing thoughts.
- Journal what you hear or see.
- Ask Him to speak to you through the Word as you pray and read, and journal that as well.
- Ask Him how He sees you and how He feels about you.

This whole workbook is about freedom.

Discussion

Read the passage from Isaiah 61:1-4 (ESV) found at the beginning of this lesson, or from your own Bible. How do you think it applies to you today?

Bringing good news.

Isaiah 61:1-4 is God's call and promise to all of us as believers — as Christ-followers. Because of the countless needs in the world, many Christian leaders adopt this passage as their life mission. It is the scripture Jesus read in the temple at the beginning of His ministry.

Be confident that you have authority over the enemy.

Look at Luke 9:1 ESV, 2 Corinthians 10:8 ESV, and 1 John 3:8b ESV. This is the key to healing prayer — to hear the voice of the Lord.

Goals of Healing Prayer

1. Learn to listen to and recognize the voice of God more often and more clearly.
2. Reach a deeper level of intimacy with the Lord that will spill over into our relationship with others.
3. Move from the frustration of getting stuck on stumbling blocks in our path to the freedom of walking fully in the gifts and calling of God.
4. Recognize any wrong thinking we've been enslaved by when we believe a lie and understand how it affects us today.
5. Know that when Jesus sets us free, we will really be free.
6. To increase our trust that He is a good God.
7. Realize how our present life can be paralyzed by our past and can overtake our future without healing prayer.
8. Realize we've been looking for help in the wrong places instead of looking to God.

The slave does not remain in the house forever; the son remains forever. So if the Son sets you free, you will be free indeed **(John 8:34b-36 ESV)**.

God Moment:

Close your eyes and listen . . .

Do not think I have forsaken you. I will not leave you suffering alone by the roadside. I know your beginning and end and all the in-between. I have a purpose and plan for you that no power of the enemy can abort. Come sit with Me and I will show you My heart for you.

Ezekiel 16:6

Jeremiah 29:11

Assignment:

1. As you sit with God, ask Him what His plans are for you; then write what you feel you are hearing.

____

____

____

2. How has the enemy tried to hinder your walk with the Lord?

____

____

____

3. When have you felt forsaken by God?

____

____

____

Final Thought

You can receive healing and freedom from the lies of the enemy.

Journal:

Lesson 2: Sabbath Rest

What Jesus intended.

God has a lot to say about completion, perfection, and rest. To model what He wanted to teach us, God rested on the seventh day after creation. This is such a foundational lesson that the number seven itself has come to represent completion and rest (Genesis 2:3).

Surely the God of the Universe was not truly tired. No, like any good parent, He was setting an example for us to follow. He was illustrating the natural rhythms of work and rest that He had set in motion. A rhythm of rest is for our own benefit in order to recharge our body, soul, and spirit. Jeremiah 17:21 (KJV) tells us we need to take this seriously: *"Thus saith the LORD; Take heed to yourselves, and bear no burden on the sabbath day, nor bring [it] in by the gates of Jerusalem;"*

Divine rhythms of rest.

If you've heard of circadian rhythms, you may think it refers only to our natural 24-hour cycles of sleep and rest when, in fact, it refers to that as well as natural weekly, monthly, and seasonal cycles throughout the earth. This is true for humans, plants, animals, and even the tides and other elements of nature. In short, our bodies are made to work best when we include a day of rest every seven days. *(see https://www.ncbi.nlm.nih.gov/pubmed/7111982)* A Sabbath rest is both a spiritual and a scientific principle. It's not a legalistic "rule" meant to please and gain favor with God, but is for our own benefit.

Discussion

Read Hebrews 4:1-11 and discuss or journal about your insights. These verses show us that we can enter God's rest spiritually every day because we don't have to earn anything from God. Jesus did the work.

Thanksgiving and rest.

As Christians, we are to live joyfully with thankfulness on the seventh day of rest because Jesus did a perfect and complete work through the cross and resurrection.

When we carry burdens continuously without rest, it can keep us from entering into the presence of God. We are weighed down with so much it is hard to focus on the Lord (Hebrews 4:9-12).

Unbelief also keeps us from entering into a Sabbath rest. Too often, we think we have to add to what Jesus has already done. At some point, we all struggle with:

- How can I be better?
- How can I do better?
- How can I be more pleasing to God?

We consciously or unconsciously think we need to do some form of works to gain favor with God, but that's a lie. This trap of human reasoning is easy to fall into when we fail to stop, rest, and focus on God and His Word rather than our own assumptions. The rest of abiding in Him becomes the fresh start of a new beginning. Since God is good, He intends everything for our good.

Discussion

Answer these questions for yourself; then discuss your insights:

What would it look like in your life to reach a deeper level of intimacy with the Lord? What are some things you can name that hinder you? How are you trying to earn God's approval by your works?

Lies we believed.

Now that we've experienced God's love, rest, and refreshment, we're prepared for Him to reveal our faulty thinking or beliefs (lies). We're going to dive more deeply into destroying the works of the devil since they wreak havoc with believers. We've been given the authority to stop many of his schemes and thereby live a more victorious, spirit-filled, and holy life.

Have you noticed how Jesus always taught by comparing spiritual truths with natural ones? 1 Corinthians 15:46.

For example

Natural:	*Spiritual:*
Light	True knowledge and presence of God (1 John 1:5)
Breath	Holy Spirit coming on the disciples (John 20:22)
Water	Holy Spirit within us (John 4:7-15, 7:37-39)

Physical birth	Spiritual birth (John 1:13, 3:3-8)
Food	Feeding on God's Word (1 Timothy 4:6; 1 Peter 2:2)

Keeping in mind the parallels between the natural and spiritual worlds, we can conclude that freedom and deliverance spiritually can be compared to freedom from nature's enemies, like pesky insects. Some harassment from the demonic can be like flies buzzing around your head—you just have to swat them away so they don't land on you. Other demonic activity is like mosquitoes that land and bite, leaving a trace of blood as evidence they've been there. And sometimes, it's more like thorns that can get embedded in your flesh and become quite sore. If you catch a "thorn" early and it's on the surface, you can take care of it yourself. If it's embedded, you will probably need help. Sometimes you can't see it hidden under the skin, but you can feel it in the soreness or pain it creates. And if it's deep enough, you may even need to see a professional to remove it. In 2 Corinthians 12:7, Paul talks about a thorn in his flesh being a messenger of Satan.

God Moment:

My child, as you sit with Me, ask Me to baptize you in my Holy Spirit. I want to fill your cup to overflowing so that you are immersed in my Spirit. Be still and picture a large cup or bucket with a rope around it. Now see it being lowered from your mind down deep into your belly or spirit. See the living water filling your cup or bucket to overflowing. Any time you want to hear My Voice allow this vessel to be lowered so that you can hear me more clearly. Out of your well of salvation can flow rivers of living water. Enter My rest.

Matthew 3:11 **Isaiah 12:3** **John 7:37**

Assignment:

1. How have you been struggling and not resting in the work of the cross?

2. What lies have you believed about God's provision for your life?

3. How do you feel the enemy has been harassing you?

Final Thought

We can stop striving because the work of the cross has provided a Sabbath rest for us.

Journal:

Lesson 3: Blessing your Conception[1]

Begin at your beginning.

Some of us know, have heard, or suspect that the circumstances or timing of our conception was less than ideal and we were somehow "a mistake" or some sort of accident. But God doesn't create accidents. He puts His very breath in our lungs. Feeling as if you were a problem for your parents is a heavy burden to bear — and a dangerous one. It can cause you to have trouble trusting His sovereignty and goodness.

The place to begin healing prayer is at your beginning in order to dismiss any lingering doubts or insecurities about your conception.

To begin uncovering Satan's lies sown so cleverly into our lives, we must begin at the beginning — the very beginning of our lives: our own conception. Did you know that every detail of your conception and gestation was ordained by God?

How you are affected by your mother's experiences before you were born.

Studies show that a baby in the womb can hear, taste, feel, know whether it is wanted or not, and can even recognize the voice of its parents. Thomas Verney, in his book, *The Secret Life of the Unborn Child,* confirms that there is active life in the womb.

The late Dr. Tom Hawkins, founder of Restoration in Christ Ministries explained:

1 This lesson corresponds to steps one and two in Section 2, beginning on page 98.

Emotions are stored in the amygdala, the emotional (e.g., fear and aggression) memory organ in the brain. It emotionally assesses data without cognitive knowledge. Many traumatic events took place at a pre-verbal age, before the child's brain had capacity for narrative (verbal) memory. Narrative memory can be triggered spontaneously or recalled voluntarily. Scientists now recognize that there is a memory apparatus in every cell of the body. This is why transplant recipients sometimes manifest characteristics of the donor.

In other words, there are issues stored in the amygdala that you have no words for because they happened at such a young age, or even pre-birth, and of which you may be unaware. However, these issues can have a great impact on your life. By asking the Holy Spirit's help in revealing these, the issues can be recognized and healed.

When we get to the Action Steps in Section 2, there will be an opportunity to pray through each trimester in the womb and examine the feelings you experienced there. You'll find that many of the negative emotions, such as fears, anxieties, rejection, etc., actually began in the womb and can follow you throughout your life, but through healing prayer, you can experience freedom from those strongholds.

Healing of past traumatic and painful memories.

Healing and deliverance come when Jesus speaks truth and shines light deep into a person's heart to bring freedom and healing to the wounded places. His words of truth will counteract the enemy's lies you have believed at any age so that forgiveness and emotional healing can come.

We have to allow Jesus to touch our painful experiences in order to bring healing. This involves listening, hearing Him speak to us, and allowing His healing love to lead us to wholeness and healing.

A word of caution: Read Luke 11:26 ***and realize that deliverance through healing prayer is a useful spiritual tool but not always advisable for those who don't know Jesus.***

Some things resulting in wounds in the womb:

- Conception in rape, incest, or adultery.
- Conception during a mother's drug-dependence.
- Mother had miscarriage or abortion before this pregnancy.
- Threatening illness of mother or baby.
- Pregnancy came at an inconvenient time in the parents' lives.
- Being the "wrong sex".
- Experiencing intense emotions from the mother caused by her own struggles.
- Being put up for adoption.
- Attempted abortion of fetus.
- Rejection or abandonment by one or both parents.

Interestingly, one psychiatric study revealed a correlation between the time of year when the mother tried unsuccessfully to abort and the time of year the later grown or semi-grown child tried to commit suicide.

Birth trauma can affect the newborn and lead to spiritual and emotional problems later in life. Some causes might be a breech birth, long labor, a C-section delivery, death of the mother during birth, umbilical cord wrapped around the neck, or an attempted abortion.

Sometimes if you feel that you were born the wrong sex or maybe you wish you were the opposite sex, you can experience shame in regard to your feelings, including a sense of rejection or a sense that you are never good enough. That shame experience can also come if there is confusion in regard to gender, such as being a tomboy or very effeminate.

If a child is adopted they may struggle with:

- Self-hatred resulting in a death wish.
- Overachieving.
- Feelings of not belonging or of being a burden.
- Fear of rejection.
- Trying to please everyone to prevent rejection.
- Resentment, defensiveness, anger, or rebellion.

The demonic usually piggybacks on trauma.

Dr. Mark Virkler, founder and president of Christian Leadership University, and Communion with God Ministries, has written more than 50 books on the topics of hearing God and spiritual healing. He explains spiritual darkness this way:

> *The Theological Dictionary of the New Testament (Vol. 2, pg. 652)* says, "In the O.T. and the N.T., *energeia* and *energew*, are used exclusively for the work of divine or demonic powers." Ephesians 2:2 speaks of living according to the prince of the power of the air, the spirit that is now "working" within the children of disobedience. Romans 7:5 uses the verb

form of the word *energew* for the "impulses of sin that are, through the law, at work (*energew*) in our members to bear fruit leading to death." Sin energy works within believers (see Romans 7) to bring them under its power and can only be overcome by the Holy Spirit who dwells within a believer (Romans 8:2).

From this explanation and the scriptures referenced, we can conclude:

- Demons are spiritual entities that desire to express themselves through humans. The fruit from this is the opposite of the fruit of the Spirit.
- Evil spirits usually gain a foothold through sin, trauma, unforgiveness, and/or offenses.
- Our agreement with the enemy empowers him to deceive us. Evil spirits are not without boundaries, so they need an open door into our lives. Just as we are bound physically by the laws of nature (that is, we can't defy gravity or be in two places at once), demons are bound by spiritual laws. We may not realize the consequences of trauma, sins, vows, unforgiveness, believing lies, or other offenses at the time we experience them, but these are the opportunities the evil one seeks that give him a legal right (spiritually speaking) to torment us, even though we are believing Christians.
- Footholds that also allow evil spirits to place someone in their grip include things like pride, deception, continuous sin, addictions, faulty belief systems, false religions, occult involvement, self-pronounced curses, fears, pornography, ungodly soul ties, unforgiveness, etc.
- Evil spirits add their demonic energy to the sin energy already present within us, which compounds the problem.

> When the wound is healed and forgiveness takes place, the enemy's power is weakened. Christian author, speaker, and evangelist Dr. Charles Kraft put it this way, "When you take out the garbage, the rats leave." Evil spirits lose their energy because they have nothing left to plug into. They no longer have power over a person. Then you are ready to get rid of the "rats."

The good news is that Jesus, through His sacrifice on the cross, has provided a way of escape. Or, using Dr. Kraft's analogy, Jesus has taken out our garbage and banished the rats, giving us a clean new life in Him. We have the power and authority, through the Holy Spirit, to withdraw the permission granted to evil spirits and take back the life Jesus intended for us to have.

Use your authority in Christ to break every demonic stronghold that has attached itself to negative emotions you have held onto. Realize that what may have begun as a coping mechanism as a child doesn't work as an adult.

God Moment

Get quiet and close your eyes. Focus in your mind's eye on Me and sense My presence. Know how much I love you, and will never leave you or forsake you. Know that I created you with purpose and destiny in mind. You are my unique creation.

Jeremiah 1:4-5
1 Peter 2:9
Psalm 139: 13-14
Genesis 1:27

Assignment

1. Picture God's hands holding a sperm in one hand and an egg in the other. See Him bringing them together to create you. What do you hear Him saying?

____

____

2. Now say, "Lord, I bless the act of my conception." How does that make you feel different?

____

____

3. What would you like your life blessed with?

____

____

Final Thought:

You were created and chosen for the purposes of God.

Journal:

Lesson 4: Generational Sins and Curses[1]

Nature or sin?

Some things we deal with can seem like a part of our nature, like they're just who we are, but they can be familial spirits passed down through the family line that have more to do with generational sins and curses rather than who God intended us to be. It's the familial, evil spirits that visit the generations, not the curses themselves.

From a spiritual warfare perspective, we need to understand that family sins repeated with each successive generation can open the door for evil spirits to become active.

Generational sins and curses are examples of demonic activity, and as Christians, we'll live a more victorious life when we learn how to get rid of these evil familial spirits assigned to our families. We can stop the pattern right here; we can repent on behalf of our ancestors and cancel the demonic assignments.

Curses can't attach to believers.

Curses cannot attach to believers, but the demons attached to the sins and curses of our family line can attack us. They have legal access through the doors that were opened for them through the sinful acts of our family line or those of our own. In other words, the blood of Jesus removed the power of curses from believers, but demons can still attack weaknesses

1 This lesson corresponds with step three in section 2, beginning on page 101.

through the generations. Galatians 3:13 says Christ redeemed us from the curse of the law by becoming a curse for us. Just like salvation, we have to appropriate it. The Israelites could believe the blood on the door would save them but they had to physically put it on the door. The actual curse is broken through the blood of Jesus, but the continued sinful acts can re-open the door for demons or familial spirits.

They look for a family member to tempt with the same familiar pattern of sin, so that when they succumb once again to the temptation, the demon gains a stronghold. They cannot just "jump" on you — you have to open the door through your own actions.

Same demonic spirit, different manifestation.

An example of this would be a spirit of addiction that could manifest in different ways such as pornography, alcoholism, gambling, theft, and so forth. The manifestation of the spirit might look different, but the fruit it produces will be the same. For instance, gambling causes a spirit of poverty, so you see the future generations struggle with poverty no matter how much money they make; it is never enough. Sexual perversion can be expressed through pornography, incest, rape, etc. Stealing can result in different ways of taking what isn't yours, like cheating someone out of something, taking financial advantage of someone, becoming a kleptomaniac, etc. You won't automatically act on these things, but if you do so when tempted, the demonic spirits will gain entry and form a stronghold.

Recognizing something's not right.

I have a friend who is very absent-minded, which results in her accidentally putting something belonging to another person in her purse as she's gathering up her own things. I know it is not intentional because she isn't even aware of it; it is more a result of not paying attention. While on a trip with her and another friend, this accidental taking of things happened more than once. I especially remember when she picked up the other friend's reading glasses and put them in her own purse. The owner of the glasses saw her do it and called her a kleptomaniac. Later, the owner of the glasses told me she really believed my friend was a compulsive kleptomaniac and was aware of taking things that weren't hers. While I've joked about it and tell others to watch their stuff when around her because she'll take it, in writing this account, I wonder if perhaps her issue has been passed down through her family by someone who actually was a thief, which would mean this absent-minded habit could be broken.

Another example of familial spirits from my own life is when my mother passed, I was holding her hand. It was a beautiful experience to see the transformation on her face. She literally looked forty-five years younger. Everyone who saw her was fascinated by the change, including the hospital staff. But for most of her life, my mother struggled with anger, jealousy, and resentment. Sometime after her passing, I began to randomly be attacked with these same angry and negative feelings, which was uncharacteristic for me. They would come out of nowhere and be very intense. I would stew in them until they finally passed.

One Sunday, while in church, I was attacked by the feelings, and I suddenly knew that it was not "just me" because I knew there was no reason to be feeling this way. I had an "aha" moment that these were not my feelings but were familial spirits from my mother, looking for a new home in me in order to express themselves. So I immediately said, "I command you to go and stop attacking me in the name of Jesus." I have never struggled with these same feelings again to that extent.

Now that attachment may have more to do with the fact that I'm her daughter than that I was holding her hand as she died, but the fact is, we have spiritual authority over familial spirits that try to attach themselves to us. We have a choice. We can say no and command them to go, if we are aware.

Generational sins and curses are examples of demonic activity, and as Christians, we'll live a more victorious life when we learn how to overcome such schemes.

Discussion

Read Exodus 20:4-6 and discuss what insight this gives you about how God views generational sins and curses.

***Seemingly inherited curses or tendencies are rooted in sin* (Deuteronomy 11:26-28).**

We talked in Workbook 4 (*Spiritual Warfare*) about how certain common sins give the enemy "legal" access to come into our lives. Both the natural and the spiritual world are ordered by God, and we can no more ignore the laws in the spiritual world than we can defy gravity and its implications in the physical world.

When we sin, knowingly or not, it gives Satan legal access to our lives. This is how we, or our ancestors, can inadvertently open doors to spiritual darkness, allowing evil spirits—or familial spirits (demonic spirits that operate within families) —to come into our lives and continue down the family line.

This is why you so often see patterns of sin repeated throughout a family, such as addictions, adultery, and so forth. Inner healing usually involves some level of spiritual warfare.

(For more information on spiritual warfare, see *Spiritual Warfare*, Workbook 4 in this series.)

We're not talking about demonic possession but rather oppression. Christians cannot be possessed.

Some evil spirits can manifest after birth, but I suspect that they could be present even as a child is being formed in the womb, particularly if the mother is struggling in the following areas while pregnant. Some of these struggles may be spiritually passed on:

- Fear
- Rebellion
- Shame
- Sexual Perversion
- Abandonment
- Rejection
- Anger
- Control
- Cult involvement, especially Masonic curses

Typically (as in my example), when these are inherited, they pop up "out of nowhere" and seem to make no sense. There seems to be no reason for the feelings, yet they can be very strong and disconcerting. If you "take the bait," that is, if you fall into sin by acting on these feelings, then you open the door to the enemy in that area.

The sins need to be renounced, and the assignments from the demonic realm need to be canceled.

Familial spirits are able to enter and oppress children at an early age because of the "legal ground" gained by the sins of their parents or others up the family line, resulting in generational curses being handed down. The legal ground the enemy has involves willful sin by an ancestor or ancestors, but it affects you.

These can be broken off and healed by repenting on behalf of your ancestor. You don't have to know who the original offender was. You'll see examples of Daniel, Nehemiah, and Ezekiel doing this for a whole nation. (See **Daniel 9**, **Nehemiah 1**, and **Jeremiah 14**, respectively.)

Another form of "inheritance" occurs when one or more of our ancestors has dedicated or committed their descendants to their particular god or occult guild, as is often done in witchcraft or Freemasonry. Here, the demons claim an "ownership" right from the womb and will do all within their power to prevent the person from hearing or understanding the Gospel. If this is from satanic worship, the healing prayer will need to be done by someone comfortable with this level of deliverance. Using the insect analogy we discussed earlier, consider this one to be like a thorn deeply embedded.

The good news is that the blood of Jesus overrides and neutralizes any other blood that has ever been shed.

Tracing Bad Fruit Back to Bad Roots.

Do you deal with emotions that have no real explanation? There may be other reasons as well, but consider whether or not you could be dealing with ancestral sin. For example, it would work like this:

> *The ancestral sin* might have been a lust of the flesh — a craving for power, sex, and/or money. These are the "Big 3" and are almost always promised by cult and occult involvement. The *bad root* is formed by cult or occult involvement by one or more of your ancestors. The *present life sin* appears in your own life as lust of the flesh, such as for power or money. All of this results in *bad fruit* — a feeling that you never have enough, you have no peace, and feel separated from God.

This hypothetical case can be traced to familial spirits passed down through a family. So, while you may have been born into a family that gave you a propensity to a particular present life sin, you are responsible for your own choices. To be free, you need to repent and cast off the demons attached to it, even though you didn't cause the root yourself.

All you may notice at first is the bad fruit, but you should be able to look closely and trace it back through sin and the bad roots it started with. Bitter roots start with some form of deception, such as believing you are justified in your thinking and behavior, etc.

Deuteronomy 29:18-20 tells us that serving other gods can result in a bitter root that bears poisonous bitter fruit (ESV, v. 20).

Deception and its negative consequences are illustrated throughout the Bible. Adam and Eve were deceived into believing God was withholding something from them, so they took what was forbidden and ate and were cast out from the presence of God (Genesis 4:8). Their sin further opened the door for the enemy to introduce them to his ways and evil practices.

Cain was so jealous of his brother that he killed him and was cast out for that sin. In a similar sibling rivalry, rather than blame himself for his own foolishness, Esau was bitter toward God because Jacob "stole" his birthright. Can you just hear the jealousy, anger, and resentment? Jacob then had to flee Esau's efforts for revenge (Genesis 25:32+).

In anger toward his son Ham, Noah cursed Ham's son Canaan, so the grandson, Cush, and great-grandson Nimrod were probably bitter toward the Lord since they were still living under Noah's curse on Canaan. Read about them in Genesis 9:22-27.

Not confessing and repenting of sin will always separate you from God.

Personal sin (Genesis 4:7)

Not all sins are ancestral of course. Most are personal, beginning in our own hearts. Personal sins are the "door" that we most frequently open to invite the enemy in to destroy us. This is especially true when the sin is repeated and becomes a pattern, leading to a lifestyle of indulging the flesh. Think of personal sins versus ancestral sins like a predisposition to some family trait or disease. For example, if obesity runs in your family, you aren't necessarily doomed to be obese as well. Your personal choices will determine whether or not you deal with the same issue. Likewise, just because an ancestor committed a sin doesn't mean we will automatically commit the same sin. But the enemy does look for a weakness and tries to get the hook in to tempt whoever in the family is most vulnerable to that sin, such as addiction. Tune in to your own thoughts and listen for things like: "It's in my genes," or, "My mother did that so…" Remember, we still have a choice about what we do. We don't have to indulge. We can swat those temptations away.

There are common areas in which we indulge our carnal

appetites, and the following list will help bring some to mind. But it isn't exhaustive. You may find others as well. Using our insect analogy, these can be mosquito bites that irritate or develop into a much more serious issue:

- Greed/Covetousness
- Jealousy/Envy
- Rebellion
- Pride (1 Timothy 3:6-7; Ezekiel 28:17)
- Lust
- Gluttony
- Gossip
- Strife
- Bitterness
- Self-Righteousness
- Criticizing, Blaming, Judging
- Unforgiveness
- Revenge

Proverbs 26:2 (ESV) says that, *"Like a sparrow in its flitting, like a swallow in its flying, a curse that is causeless does not alight."* This tells us that the enemy needs an open door. He can't attack you without a reason.

So if you're being attacked, to determine the reason, you'll need to ask yourself, "Is it my sin or generational curses as a result of ancestral sin? Could these things I struggle with stem from bitter roots that are ancestral, or something personal? Is there a pattern in my life? For example, a pattern of financial struggles, job losses, sickness, bad relationships, addictions, anger, unforgiveness, or hate?" Typically, some form of deception, like believing a lie, causes the most bitter roots.

Hebrews 12:15 instructs us to examine ourselves in light of the grace of God, to keep from becoming bitter or defiled. *"Looking diligently lest any man fail of the grace of God; lest any root of bitterness springing up trouble you, and thereby many be defiled;"*

Anger toward God can make you rebellious, bitter toward Him, and determined to go your own way. It causes an anti-Christ spirit, a struggle with commitment and faithfulness to the Lord. You will feel "cast out" of the presence of God. This can cause the bitter root, which results in fruit of jealousy, anger, resentment, perversion, etc., throughout your life and circumstances.

Other examples.

A *bad root* can start when you are offended by something you believe God has or hasn't done, which reveals a spirit of judgment and/or pride. The *present sin* in your life is unforgiveness, blaming God or others (Hebrews 12:15 ESV). This *results in the bad fruit* of bitterness and resentful anger toward God that causes you to withdraw from spending time with Him or in fellowship with others. You begin to have doubt, unbelief, and especially bondage, which is actually one of the bad fruits of nearly every sin.

Personal wrong choices.

The *bad root* may start with pride of life, or lust of the eyes, which would lead to *sins* including love of money, coveting, jealousy, and insecurity (1 Timothy 6:10). This would yield *resulting bad fruit,* including a workaholic lifestyle that's born from a sense of never having enough, causing neglect of others and yourself. Another result may be falling into bondage to debt, insecurity, pride, selfishness, loneliness, or stinginess.

If the *bad root* is a religious spirit, it could have come from misunderstandings or bad teaching. It will result in *sin,* including no real relationship with God, hypocrisy between what you say vs. what you do, such as putting form and ritual ahead of trust and growth in Christ. The *resulting bad fruit* will be strongholds such as performance, manipulation, bondage, and superstition. (To understand more on breaking strongholds, see page 110.)

The good news is that it works the other way around too. Good roots become good fruit in your life.

Good roots produce good fruit.

You can see from Isaiah 11:1 and 10 that good roots result in blessings and freedom from bondage. When we are rooted in Christ, we produce good fruit. (Also 2 Corinthians 3:17).

We see in Galatians 3:13 that Christ redeemed us from the curse of the law. We can also have confidence through Matthew 3:10 that He wants to lay an ax to the root of sin in our lives.

Galatians 5:22-23 and John 15:5 remind us that He is the vine, we are the branches. We bear or carry good fruit that others can eat.

See 2 Kings 19:30 — We take root downward and bear fruit upward when we are rooted and grounded in Him.

Remember, legal ground for the enemy is sin committed by us or an ancestor, but there is victory available in that the blood of Christ overrides that sin and the blood of anything else that has been shed.

God Moment

My beloved, come into My garden and I will help you see the good seeds that I want to plant in your heart. These will replace the weeds that are the result of your self-effort. Those represent false fronts you present to the world. Together, let's pull up the weeds to make room for the good seeds that will produce good fruit.

Song of Solomon 4:12-15

Galatians 5:16

Assignment

1. What are some things you deal with that you blame on others?

2. What behavior in your life do you believe is "in your genes"?

3. How have you developed bad fruit in your life as a result of this?

Final Thought

You can choose to sow good seeds that produce life.

Lesson 5: Soul Ties[1]

The term *soul ties* is commonly believed to describe how two souls are knit together spiritually. We don't find this term anywhere in the Bible specifically, however, we do see references to "their souls are knit" together, becoming "one flesh," etc., so the basic concept of soul ties is clearly evident.

The Bible refers to David and Jonathan's relationship in 1 Samuel 18:1 as the soul of Jonathan being knit with the soul of David, and Jonathan loved him as his own soul. Their relationship seems to be a healthy soul tie and a result of close friendship.

But he who is joined to the Lord becomes one spirit with him. (1 Corinthians 6:17 ESV) describes a Godly soul tie. *Our soul has escaped as a bird from the snare of the fowler; the snare is broken, and we have escaped* (Psalms 124:7) describes breaking free of an ungodly soul tie, so soul ties can be either healthy (godly) or unhealthy. Soul ties are not automatically bad but since we are addressing the need for healing we will primarily be discussing ungodly soul ties here rather than healthy ones.

An ungodly soul tie is a toxic relationship with someone who needs something from you and tries to control you. Many times you get caught in a trap because you think you can save them.

Any sex outside of marriage creates an ungodly soul tie, as does an unhealthy relationship of any kind where we try to control someone or allow him or her to control us. It is hard to leave a relationship when there are toxic emotions involved.

1 This lesson corresponds with step six in section 2, beginning on page 112.

A soul tie can be an inexplicably powerful emotional bond to another person. The bond can be formed through a physical, spiritual, social, or emotional connection.

Codependent relationships are toxic soul ties and can happen easily when someone is a people pleaser. Codependent relationships involve using other people to meet your own emotional needs in a selfish and destructive way.

We can find soul ties in a number of areas of life and life circumstances. For example, soul ties can be found in marriage and family relationships, business, sex, friendship, and even with pets. Prolonged grief, manipulation, pride, and gossip can all also lead to unhealthy soul ties.

Soul ties between married couples coming together should be healthy. However, an unhealthy soul tie can allow one spouse to manipulate and control the other, and the other spouse may be unaware of what is going on or, even if they realize it, allow the unhealthy cycle to continue.

Vows, commitments, and agreements.

Vows are known to bind the soul **(Numbers 30:2)**, marriage itself consists of vows and binds people together **(Ephesians 5:31)**, so vows and commitments can be a means to create a healthy, godly soul tie.

An ungodly soul tie can be formed with almost any person, place, thing, or event. For example, even with a rock group by becoming obsessed with their music. That would explain a strong pull towards certain music that feels almost irresistible.

Ungodly sexual soul ties.

Dr. Daniel Amen writes in his book, *Change your Brain, Change your Life*, "Whenever a person is sexually involved with another person, neurochemical changes occur in both their brains that encourage limbic, emotional bonding. Limbic bonding is the reason casual sex doesn't work for most people on a whole mind and body level. Two people may decide to have sex, 'just for the fun of it,' yet something is occurring on another level that they might not have decided on at all: Sex is enhancing an emotional bond between them whether they want it or not. One person, often the woman, is bound to form an attachment and will be hurt when a casual affair ends. One reason it is usually the woman who is hurt most is that the female limbic system is larger than the males." *This is a science-based definition of what we are calling soul ties.*

Many Christians think 2 Corinthians 6:14 merely admonishes Christians not to marry non-believers, but it actually means much more. Just as the traditional marriage vows refer to "the two become one," so sexual relationships outside the bonds of marriage (whether consensual or not) create a lasting "yoke" or soul tie that needs to be renounced. It can happen in other instances as well. Being unequally yoked to someone else can happen through an unhealthy emotional, psychological, sexual, or spiritual soul tie. To be free, the connection needs to be severed spiritually. It might be from the trauma of abuse, rape, or any pre-marital sex.

We are not to be allied or identified with unbelievers. When you are wrongly yoked with someone, their conduct and opinions strongly influence or control you. Scriptures addressing this issue are: 2 Corinthians 6:14, Leviticus 19:19, Mark 10:8, and 1 Corinthians 6:16.

Soul ties can be with things or places too.

An unholy soul tie does not have to be with a person but can be formed with addictive substances, or created through oaths and ties to certain clubs or associations, departed spirits from miscarriages, abortions, or anyone who has died that you "communicate" with. These are not the ones who have died, but are deceiving familial spirits who knew all about the person and can therefore masquerade as your departed loved one.

Soul ties can even be caused by unhappy or painful memories tied to a specific location where one suffered trauma or sadness. This would cause you to have demonic attachments and avoid that place because of how it makes you feel to go there.

Soul ties between fornicators (sex partners outside of marriage) can draw an abused woman to a man that in the natural realm she would hate and even run from. With a soul tie involved, she runs to him even though he doesn't love her and treats her like dirt. This can also happen in an abusive marriage. In the demonic world, unholy soul ties can serve as bridges between two people to pass demonic garbage back and forth.

Sex involves spirit, soul, and body.

As Dr. Amen explained earlier, bonds like this blossom after sexual intercourse. Sex involves spirit, soul, and body. Anytime you have sex with a person, you bond with them. I've read it described that sex is like gluing two pieces of wood together and the next day ripping them apart. Of course, it doesn't split exactly where it was glued; wood from one board remains on the other board and vice versa. A part of your sex partner stays with you for the rest of your life. Think about what that looks like when you bond with multiple partners. You're creating lifelong bonds through sexual encounters, but with those whom you only have a short-term relationship.

Ungodly sexual soul ties always involve a seducing spirit, which opens the door to perverse spirits. The bond remains long after the relationship is over, leading both partners longing for wholeness. Unhealthy soul ties take place from a physical act with no emotional or spiritual connection, but it does open a spiritual channel, good or bad. One of the partners involved might even find themselves longing for the other person even though they don't like them. Usually the woman might give herself to someone expecting that the intensely intimate act would create a bond leading to a deeper commitment in the relationship. But she soon discovers that her partner was taking advantage of her need for intimacy and used her vulnerability merely to satisfy a sexual desire. This can lead to resentment toward that person and anger or depression within oneself.

When two people have sex before marriage, they often justify it by saying the covenant vows are only a formality. Or they might live together having sex outside of the lifelong commitment of marriage. Perhaps later they decide they don't want to live in a covenant relationship and break up. They don't realize how deeply they hurt each other as their souls are ripped apart, much like the pieces of wood we mentioned earlier. It tears the very fabric of their being.

Signs that you have an unhealthy soul tie.

You may realize you have an unhealthy soul tie if you are in a physically, emotionally, or spiritually abusive relationship, or a combination of all three aspects of abuse. But you may have a hard time leaving and severing the toxic connection. This is extremely common. Statistically, many women go back to their abusers as many as seven times after initially trying to leave. Perhaps you've left a relationship, but you still think about the other person obsessively. Whenever you do anything, make a decision or have a conversation, you feel like this person is with you or watching you.

It's not always a sexual relationship that yokes a person.

Soul ties can be from having an unhealthy, controlling, or codependent relationship with a family member, a controlling spiritual leader, toxic-church experience, "mentor," friend, or even a pet.

A toxic example.

I have a friend who grew up believing the lie that she was a lesbian. She never acted on it, however, after becoming a Christian, she got involved with a pastor's wife who kissed her. I don't think the relationship went beyond that physically, but through that experience, a soul tie was formed.

My friend later decided to move to the U.S. to attend a Christian Bible school. While there, as she would get ready in the morning, she would see the pastor's wife's face beside her looking back at her in the mirror.

At some point a speaker came to the school that had just been speaking in my friend's country. She heard about my friend, and as they began to talk, my friend told her what was happening. The speaker asked my friend if this person had given her anything. The answer was yes; she had given her clothes suitable for our southern climate and a set of sheets that she was sleeping on. The speaker told her she needed to get rid of those gifts to be free of these manifestations caused by a "familiar spirit" and to break the soul tie between them. After my friend did this, the manifestations stopped.

When you have sex with someone, a soul tie is created, and you'll find you can hardly keep yourself from visualizing the person you now have a soul tie with. You might even take on the negative traits of that person and carry their offenses with you, whether you agree with them or not. I've seen people completely defy logic as they adamantly defend their right to stay in a relationship with a person even though it is negatively affecting or even destroying the key relationships in their lives. If you're in a situation like this, you may find yourself having simultaneous experiences and moods as the person your soul is tied to. This can include illnesses, accidents, addictions, and more. 1 Corinthians 6:15 confirms this when it tells us: *do you not know that the one who joins himself to a prostitute is one body with her? For he says, the two shall become one flesh.*

A largely misunderstood concept or fact is that soul ties are not just about sex, though sex certainly can strengthen or enhance a soul tie. But just as the name implies, a soul tie is a strong connection with someone or something that is deeply embedded in your soul. They do not have to be romantic relationships.

Breaking unhealthy soul ties.

So, once you've realized you have an unhealthy soul tie, how do you get out of it? First, of course, you have to acknowledge that there is a problem in the relationship. Since your soul is comprised of your mind, will, and emotions, when you have a soul tie with another person, your mind, will, and emotions become enmeshed with that of the other person. Decide you're going to do something about it and take action. An important part of breaking a soul tie is repentance of sins that were committed to cause the soul tie and forgiveness.

Prayer: *"In the name of Jesus, I repent of and renounce all sinful and unholy acts with __________. I break any ungodly soul ties and demonic attachments connected to this relationship. In the name of Jesus, I command all familiar spirits and any other spirits attached to these ties to leave me now. Lord, I thank you for delivering me. Amen.*

Another important thing to do is remove any physical objects that might link you to a person in a sinful way. This might mean gifts given to you by them representing a sinful relationship or photos you're keeping if looking at them draws you to the person in an unhealthy way, as well as anything else that causes you to visualize a sinful connection between yourself and the other person. Repent of any vows made with that person that would hold you to them. Proverbs 21:23 says that the tongue has the ability to bring the soul great trouble and bondage. Verbal commitments need to be undone verbally. Forgiveness is important.

Ask Jesus to wash and restore the parts of each other's hearts that were fractured. For example:

Prayer: *"I ask you Father, in the name of Jesus to bring back any torn and broken places in my heart and soul as a result of these relationships. I repent of allowing someone else to take from me what wasn't theirs to have. I ask you to completely restore my soul. I'll let go of anything I've held onto regarding the relationship. I ask you to forgive me as I forgive them."*

If a core part of yourself split off, ask God when it happened and to bring it back. This commonly happens when a child is abused.

Sometimes you need to ask the Lord to sever any ties concerning locations or objects. These could be from a clinic where a person had an abortion, it could be from a location that represented sinful sexual relationships, abuse, or other trauma.

God Moment

Beloved, come confidently into My Presence. When you have confessed your sin, feel My love and forgiveness. Know that my Son Jesus has already paid the price for your sin, and He is all you need. Bring to Me all your hurts and wounds and allow Me to heal all the broken places in your heart. I will restore all the enemy has stolen from you.

Assignment

1. Explain how any unhealthy relationships caused spiritual problems in your life.

____

____

2. Ask the Lord if there are any spirits attached to these relationships lingering in your thoughts and heart. Then, just to be sure, pray, "in the name of Jesus, I command all familiar spirits and any other spirits attached to these ties to leave me. Thank you Lord for delivering me."

____

____

3. Ask God what you have given someone that wasn't theirs to have. Journal what He shows you.

____

____

Joel 2:25

Jeremiah 30:17

John 10:10

Final thought:

Repentance and forgiveness bring healing and restoration.

Lesson 6: Inner Vows[1]

Powerful emotions.

Powerful emotions like anger, hurt, or shame can be scary, causing one to feel if they give in to the emotion (i.e., fully experience the emotions), they might never be able to recover. The problem is, when you shut down one emotion, often the other emotions get shut down or amplified. This can sometimes result in having difficulty allowing any emotions to surface at all. Give yourself some time, and rely on the Holy Spirit for guidance. This may be an instance when you'd want to consider counseling as a follow-up to your healing prayer experience (Colossians 3:8; 1 Timothy 2:8; James 1:19-20; Isaiah 41:10).

Inner vows.

Inner vows often grow from powerful emotions and are like contracts or promises we make about ourselves. They will come to pass whether they are intentional or not, remembered or not, spoken aloud or not. Inner vows represent us choosing our will over God's and need to be confessed, repented of, and canceled before we can experience the fullness of all God has for us. See Psalm 89:34; Mark 11:23; James 5:12; Proverbs 20:25.

Matthew 5:33-37 (NLT) says *You have also heard that our ancestors were told, you must not break your vows, you must carry out the vows you make to the Lord. But I say do not make any vows, just say a simple yes I will, or no I won't. Anything beyond this is from the evil one.*

---

1 This lesson corresponds with step seven in section 2, beginning on page 117..

An inner vow is a self-directed and self-focused promise that we make to ourselves in response to our difficulty, frustration, or pain.

Inner vows happen when something in a person rises up to protect themselves and those they love from a repeat performance; they affect the mind and the heart. Instead of trusting God to protect them, the person thinks it's their own responsibility to protect themselves or someone else. **Psalms 91:14-15** says, *Because he loves me, says the LORD, I will rescue him; I will protect him, for he acknowledges my name. He will call upon me, and I will answer him; I will be with him in trouble…* Inner vows are not always bad things to want, but the problem is that we are trying to do it in our own strength and not by relying on the Lord.

We forget the inner vows made in childhood, but they can be more powerful than the ones we have made as adults. Words have spiritual power. The enemy will empower the words we speak that are against God's will for our lives so that they hold us in bondage.

Sowing and reaping.

Depending on our own strength is always the problem with an inner vow. We should say instead, "Lord, with your help I will …" versus the "I will …" which is in our own strength. These inner vows have the power to change the course of our lives and prevent us from becoming all God wants us to be.

Inner vows can result in outcomes for our lives that we would never have consciously chosen. An inner vow causes us to feel driven to act in ways that we ourselves often don't even understand. If we trust God to protect us, we can rest in the knowledge that He has our best interest at heart, and He will direct our path.

Inner vows usually involve judgment. We need to forgive, extend grace to others as well as ourselves, and lean on God's strength rather than our own. Only God knows someone's heart in a matter and why they act the way they do. Bitter root judgments will produce bad fruit. Perhaps you had a father or mother who was an alcoholic, so you vowed never to be like them. You might not become an alcoholic, but you will likely have some other addiction.

The simple truth is that we become what we behold, that is, what we focus on. In the negative sense of this truth, if we focus on NEVER becoming like our mother, she is EXACTLY who we will become. The cliché is often true: *"Mirror, mirror on the wall ... I am my mother after all."*

Focus on Jesus and become like Him first and foremost.

An inner vow is usually the result of an unhealthy relationship or situation, unfulfilled expectations, and/or unmet needs. Only God can protect us and show us what He has in mind for our future and how to deal with life's disappointments and pain. When we rely on our own limited strength, we fail, but when we turn to God, we succeed.

Why would we make inner vows and try to control our own destiny rather than allow God's plan for our lives? We are deceived if we believe we can control anything.

Inner vows are often made in response to our judgment of others. Vows such as:

- I will never be like her/him.
- I will never allow anyone to hurt me like that again.
- I will never trust anyone.
- I will never let anyone get too close.
- I will never let anyone control me.
- I will never be vulnerable.
- I will never trust an authority figure again.
- I will not cry again.
- I will prove I am worthy and lovable.

Vows are a result of trying to control our own lives while judging, not forgiving, and not trusting God to protect us (Romans 2:1).

Inner vows cause you to construct a wall around your heart, which hardens your heart. They also cause us to become hostage to our past even though our circumstances have changed drastically. Inner vows are still working in our subconscious mind even if we stop thinking about them consciously.

Examples of inner vows from being wounded in a marriage:

- I will not trust my spouse again.
- I will not let my spouse control our relationship.
- I will not allow myself to be vulnerable.
- I will not let my spouse hurt me again, so I will harden my heart.
- I will not give affection to or receive affection from my spouse again.
- I will not desire my spouse again.

Inner vows produce unhealthy fruit. Some symptoms of inner vows could include anger, anxiety, unrealistic expectations, compulsive behavior, hatred, and stubbornness. You might have strong reactions to certain triggers. They can cause you to live out of fear rather than love and have false expectations.

Unmet needs can result in making inner vows about not feeling loved, validated, accepted, not feeling safe, or that your opinions count. We also make "I will" vows such as: I will be successful, I will be loving to others, always look a certain way, keep my mouth shut and not give opinions, etc.

These might not be bad things, but as we said earlier, your vows result in relying on your own power instead of God's.

Ask Him to help you to trust others, be authentic, and be unafraid of being hurt. Surrender harmful things to Him, find your identity in Him, and truly forgive.

God Moment

My child, trust Me with your future and surrender to Me control in all areas of your life. My plans for you far exceed anything you can imagine or hope for. Give Me your hurts and fears, and I will give you peace. Believe in My love for you and listen to My Spirit as I show you what to let go of so you can enter into My rest.

Assignment

1. How have powerful emotions caused you to make inner vows?

___

___

2. What are the vows and judgments you have made?

___

___

3. How have these inner vows hardened your heart and affected your mind, will, emotions, and body?

___

___

Ezekiel 36:26
Matthew 5:22
Psalms 18:2
Jeremiah 17:5
Proverbs 20:25

Final thought:

Give God control of your life; His plan for you is better than yours.

Lesson 7: Word Curses and Negative Beliefs[1]

Word curses.

In biblical times, a man's word was a binding contract. The Bible says that words can bring spiritual life (blessings) or spiritual death (curses). Proverbs 18:21 says *Death and life are in the power of the tongue and those who love it will eat its fruits.*

Word curses are negative declarations we've said about ourselves, or things others have said to or about us that we've taken to heart in a hurtful or negative way. Any labels or names we've put on ourselves, or that others have spoken about us, become curses when we come into agreement with the negative words or labels. It causes negative beliefs about oneself. The reverse, by the way, is also true: negative beliefs can bring on word curses. They go hand-in-hand (Proverbs 12:18).

God's word is powerful.

Genesis 1:4-10 says, *"And God said..."* at least eight different times as He created each part of the world. He *spoke* the world into existence. The same Holy Spirit who was involved in creation lives in us. Hence, our words can be a powerful spiritual force. Jesus said in Mark 11:23 that if anyone says to this mountain, go, throw yourself in the sea and does not doubt in their heart but believes that what they say will happen, it will be done for them.

Since the power of life or death is in our tongue we should be careful what we speak about or over other people, making

1 This lesson corresponds with steps eight and nine in section 2, beginning on page 116.

sure our words edify and produce life. Proverbs 12:6 says our words have the power to build up or tear down. Negative words pierce the heart, and false labels put on us can be taken to heart and believed to be true. Sometimes our parents unwittingly say things to us that plant lies in our heart.

Word curses open the door for demonic torment. They gain power over us when we come into agreement with the words spoken. The good news is that we can replace those lies with what Jesus says about us and about who we are in Him. The blood of Jesus has the power to break every curse ever spoken over us, whether intentional or not. Galatians 3:13-14 says He redeemed us from the curse of the law by becoming a curse for us. John 10:10 says it's the enemy who comes to steal, kill, and destroy. The provision for being set free is provided by Christ, but just like salvation, we have to appropriate it because it doesn't happen automatically.

Words have spiritual power and are a real force in the world (Proverbs 11:11). Once they are released into the atmosphere, you can't get them back. Word curses are the opposite of a spoken blessing. Most people think that word curses only come from witches, etc., but they are usually from people close to us. They have the most power when spoken by a parent, sibling, spouse, close friend, teacher, coach, and especially someone with spiritual authority like a parent or pastor. Many times it is not intentional, but the words still have power over the person. It's common for evil spirits to attach to these word curses because they open the door to the demonic.

A personal example was when I won a superlative in my senior year of high school. I was awarded "Most Witty" in my yearbook. When I proudly showed my mother, she said, "What does that mean? Most Stupid?" After that, she said she was just kidding. But it was too late because those words had already pierced my heart. Even though I knew I was smart, at times I struggled with feelings of appearing stupid. This is further proof that the tongue is a spiritual weapon to be used for building up or tearing down, and we should think before we speak.

James said that the tongue is *an unruly evil, full of deadly poison* (James 3:8). He goes on to say this: *With it we bless our God and Father, and with it we curse men, who have been made in the image of God. Out of the same mouth proceed blessing and cursing. My brethren, these things ought not to be so* (James 3:9-10).

Words can bring life or death, healing or hurt, blessing or cursing. The saying that "Sticks and stones can break my bones but words can never hurt me" is a lie. When we believe a word curse spoken over us and agree with it, the lie takes root and becomes a supernatural force that brings harm and destruction. Negative beliefs go hand in hand with word curses. Self-imposed word curses present a very damaging inroad for torment.

Curses form in the heart.

When someone hates another person, he or she will wish misfortune on the other person. If we realize we are doing this or have done this concerning someone, we need to repent and speak blessings over them instead.

The words of the reckless pierce like swords, but the tongue of the wise brings healing. (Proverbs 12:18 NIV)

Objects and places can also be cursed through sin and spoken curses. Deuteronomy 7:26 ESV *And you shall not bring an abominable thing into your house and become devoted to destruction like it. You shall utterly detest and abhor it, for it is devoted to destruction.*

If you feel you have been dealing with certain issues and can't get victory, you may have objects in your home that have had curses placed on them. Especially if you have noticed some demonic manifestations happening that you cannot explain. I have a friend whose daughter was having nightmares, and I noticed a doll in her room that had been brought back from Africa. It was very pretty, dressed in white and looked completely innocent, but after getting rid of it, the nightmares stopped. Many of these innocent souvenirs from other countries have a curse placed on them by those who made them. I read that Buddhist monks put curses of homelessness on the soldiers who came to Vietnam. Whether that's true or not, many are homeless, and there seems to be a curse of birth defects on their descendants from the effects of Agent Orange.

In the Old Testament, Balaam was hired by Balak to curse Israel, but God wouldn't allow him to curse them. However, he did tell them to trap Israel by getting them to commit adultery with their women, who would then lure them into worshiping their gods (Numbers 25:3). He knew that the only way Israel could be defeated was through her own sin. God had forbidden them to worship other gods, so they brought a curse on themselves through their disobedience. They had to willingly open the door for the curse. God says that a curse without a cause cannot light. (Proverbs 26:2).

Ask God if there is any open door in your life. If there is, confess it, repent, and break any subsequent curse as a result.

The key to healing and deliverance is to forgive those who have intentionally or unintentionally placed curses on us and speak blessings over them and ourselves. Matt 5:44 *For I tell you, love your enemies and pray for those who persecute you.*

The Holy Spirit is activated to perform God's work when we speak the Word of God over our lives and situations.

Prophetic words are blessings and the opposite of curses. Scripture reminds us of the importance of keeping God's Words, promises, and prophetic words before our eyes. In 1 Timothy 1:18, the Apostle Paul told Timothy, *This charge I commit to you, son Timothy, according to the prophecies previously made concerning you, that by them you may wage the good warfare.* Psalms 119:11 reads, *Thy word have I hid in mine heart, that I might not sin against thee.* In Proverbs 6, the young man is told to pay special attention to the words of his father and mother, to bind them around his neck, and they will keep him from wayward women.

Christian teacher and author Graham Cooke has said that the promises and words that God has spoken to us have to become as real in our hearts as they are in His. Taking the time to mull over, meditate upon, and fix these in our hearts causes faith to build around each prophetic word and promise.

Negative beliefs.

Then he touched their eyes, saying According to your faith be it done to you. (Matthew 9:29, ESV).

And Jesus said to him, "'If you can!' All things are possible for one who believes." (Mark 9:23, ESV).

Sometimes we confuse negative beliefs with inner vows but negative beliefs are false beliefs or conclusions you believe about yourself, God, your situation, your expectations about your circumstances, or your future. They control your life when not replaced with God's promises. We must learn to take those thoughts captive 2 Corinthians 10:5.

Negative beliefs mean we are not agreeing with God.

They cause us not to trust God and to deny that He has our best interests at heart. Negative beliefs also cause us to focus on what God is *not* rather than what God *is*, fostering beliefs such as:

- I am unattractive.
- I am clumsy.
- I am accident-prone.
- I am dumb.
- I cannot be a good reader.
- I cannot be a good speaker.
- I will always be a day late and a dollar short.
- I will always have money troubles.
- I will always be unemployed.
- I will always be different and an outcast.
- I am a loser.
- I am less than others.
- I have more problems than others.
- I am ugly.
- I will always be overweight.
- I will never trust that there will be enough.
- I will never be safe financially.
- I will never be good enough (especially if you believe you were a mistake and the opposite sex was preferred)

Ask God to help you to trust Him. Surrender your negative beliefs to Him and find your identity in Him.

Discussion

Who does God say you are?

Deuteronomy 7:6, John 15:15-16, 1 Peter 2:9 and Psalms 139

God Moment

Beloved, I suffered for you and took your punishment on Myself so you would not live under a curse. My wounds were for your salvation — spirit, soul, and body. You are mine. Let Me pour the healing balm of Gilead over the wounded places in your heart where the darts of the enemy have caused pain and suffering. Agree with who I say you are and allow My peace to wash over you.

Assignment

1. What are some harmful words spoken by you and about you?

____

____

2. How has this caused you to have negative beliefs about yourself?

____

____

3. What would God want to replace those with?

____

____

Song of Solomon 4:1
Galatians 2:20
1 Peter 2:9-10

Final thought:

You are God's creation and His special treasure; only believe what He says about you.

Lesson 8: Releasing the Poison with Theo Therapy and Theophostic[1]

Theo therapy — empty chair.

Theo therapy comes from two Greek words meaning *God's healing*. Theo therapy is a technique used for expressing pent up feelings toward someone who has hurt you as if they were present even though they are not. The Empty Chair is a technique used in Theo therapy to help people receive closure and/or help empower victims. It comes out of the Gestalt counseling style and was invented by Fritz and Laura Perls in the 1950s. It can be a very powerful tool for some people in their healing. It can be especially helpful for abuse victims or those who have lost a loved one unexpectedly.

Abuse or grief victims imagine the abuser or lost loved one is sitting in an empty chair. They look at the empty chair and say anything that is on their heart to the empty chair. Some individuals, after they have spoken to the empty chair, then switch chairs and verbalize a response from the abuser or lost loved one, telling themselves words they have longed to hear. They might say things like, "I'm sorry I hurt you," or even, "I love you, and I'm proud of you." This works especially well if they have needed to hear these words and their abuser or loved one was unwilling or unable to say these things to them. (from Sharon Sitler, Licensed Clinical Psychologist)

This is the first step I ever took to experience inner healing for myself. I was in my mid-thirties when a young psychologist

1 This lesson corresponds with steps four, ten, eleven and twelve in section 2, beginning on pages 103, 119, 120, and 121 respectively.

took me through the process. I was unaware I had pent up anger toward my dad for something that happened to me when I was about twelve or thirteen. As a result, I was taking it out on my husband. I hadn't always done this, but when he would come up behind me to hug me I would freeze.

This was such a painful memory that I could never speak of it until that day. When I would try to share it, I would cry so hard I couldn't talk. During the ministry time, I told my dad, who wasn't actually there since he had passed away a few years before, that he was stupid. I realized that I thought all men were pretty much stupid. When I shared the experience with my husband, he said he could tell I felt that way about men — which shows he was, and is, a lot smarter than I gave him credit for! This ministry time only took about fifteen minutes, but it changed my marriage, my life, and began my journey of praying with others to experience inner emotional healing.

Theo therapy prayer does for your emotions what you'd naturally do for yourself in the physical: for example, if you were riding a bike, fell off and didn't ever clean the wound, it would heal with dirt trapped inside. Infection would result and spread throughout your body. It is the same with emotional wounds. Going back to the memory will open the wound, expressing emotions will clean it out, forgiving is the antiseptic, and releasing it to God is like stitching up the wound so healing can begin.

Theo therapy prayer does for your emotions what you'd naturally do for yourself in the physical.

Imagine the person that hurt you is sitting across from you. Then verbalize all your feelings of anger, hatred, resentment, hurt, etc., that you have toward this person. When you've finished getting all your feelings out and expressed, forgive them, forgive yourself for the feelings, and stop blaming God for allowing it, recognizing that God is not responsible for the evil in our world. Then release the person who wounded you to the Lord. This could take a few minutes or an hour or more.

Discussion

Is there something that needs to be said to someone in your life, either in person or using the theo therapy empty chair technique?

Theophostic — God's light.

The word theophostic means *God's light.* When a person has painful traumatic memories from past wounds whether they be physical, emotional, from sexual abuse, a death, an accident, or a divorce, etc., they usually can't be free until they go through healing prayer and deliverance from any demonic attachments.

For healing and deliverance from the lies embedded in these memories, it is necessary to allow the Lord Jesus to come into these painful places and shed His light to reveal the lies and replace them with His truth. When sexual trauma happens at a very young age, the child will disassociate, which means that a part of their soul splits and another part or someone else takes over in order to cope with what happened. The demonic always "piggybacks" on or is empowering the alternate personality. This explains why some believe that alternate personalities are demons and others believe they are part of the victim's soul; both are true. Different identities, or controlling alters, usually have demons attached.

To be free involves honesty and transparency.

It is necessary for the one who has experienced trauma to give the Holy Spirit permission to visit a painful memory. That can be hard when the act was so humiliating and horrendous that the person can't imagine the Lord watching.

A person's emotional pain is usually rooted in the past. This might not be from sexual trauma; it could be from something else like abusive emotional or physical treatment by another person. It could be extreme criticism from a parent or teacher or bullying by friends. The memories are usually based on lies planted in the person's heart at the time. The lies usually have to do with the person's identity or self-worth.

It's important to hear Jesus speak truth.

We invite Jesus to come alongside the person to speak truth in a painful memory. Jesus will bring comfort and speak truth to replace the lie that was believed as a result of the trauma — there is always a lie attached. It might be accusations like it was your fault, you're dirty, there must be something wrong with you, you wanted it to happen, you didn't get something right. Or it could be things like you were abandoned and nobody cares, nobody loves you, if anyone finds out they won't like you, etc.

False beliefs and triggers.

The emotional pain that haunts many people's lives, including Christians, is rooted in false beliefs associated with past experiences rather than what is happening in the present. Satan is often the source of those lies, while Jesus is the source of the truth that dispels them. (John 8:44,14:6,18:37).

When a person has a strong reaction (trigger) that has no explanation to a current situation, it is usually rooted in a past experience causing the reaction to be out of proportion to what is happening. Ed Smith, the founder of Theophostic ministries, argues that such primal traumatic experiences and their false interpretations are registered in the right side of our brains, while our ability to understand data intellectually and objectively is the function of the left side of our brains. He believes this explains why he was having no success convincing adult survivors of sexual abuse that they were no longer in danger: in order to be delivered from the emotional power of those lies, the survivors would need to learn the truth experientially, in a manner similar to how the lies were implanted in their minds originally.

Discussion

What are the things that trigger you?

The Theophostic Ministry process is a process of drifting back from memory to memory with the goal of locating the original lie, and asking Jesus to replace it with His truth.

The key to freedom is in revisiting the memory where the person first felt the emotions and allowing Jesus to replace the lies with His truth. The past is replaced with the present Romans 12:2 and helps to renew the mind and change the thinking from being a victim to being a victor.

If you are leading and praying for someone this way, it is important to remember not to plant memories in order to help them get where you think they need to go. Do not use guided imagery or tell them what you think they need to know. Allow the Holy Spirit to lead them and listen to the Holy Spirit yourself to know how to pray for them. Always invite the Holy Spirit in to lead and show the person what they need to see. If, after praying, the person isn't free from the emotion that accompanies the particular memory, there is probably one further back in their past they need to visit. For instance, if the emotion is shame, and they are not free of it, then you need to go back further in their past to when they first experienced this feeling. When you are finished, the person should be experiencing peace and/or feeling "lighter."

Always make sure when doing healing prayer with others that what they hear and see Jesus doing lines up with scripture.

Recalling the warning inherent in Luke 11:26, we want to be sure that, along with our spiritual housecleaning, we are asking God for a fresh filling of His Holy spirit, leaving no room for the enemy to return.

A fresh infilling of the Holy Spirit.

Before you ever end a session of healing prayer, either by yourself or with others, always end by asking for a fresh infilling of the Holy Spirit, and pray blessing from scripture over everyone praying or present during the session. Using these or your own words, pray: "*Father, I thank you for the work You've done here today and ask that you fill the empty places that have been swept clean with the fruit of Your Spirit as listed in* Galatians 5:22-23*: love, joy, peace, forbearance, kindness, faithfulness, gentleness and self-control. Thank you Lord, in Jesus' name. Amen.*

After your prayer, it's also a good idea to read aloud scriptures of blessing for yourself and those with you, especially those that relate to you, God's promises, and the specific situations or circumstances you've been praying about. See Discussion section below for examples.

Discussion

Read and discuss the following scriptures of blessing. How do you feel about blessing yourself and others regularly?

There is therefore now no condemnation for those who are in Christ Jesus. For the law of the Spirit of life has set you free in Christ Jesus from the law of sin and death. (Romans 8:1-2 ESV).

But the fruit of the Spirit is love, joy, peace, patience, kindness, goodness, faithfulness, gentleness, self-control; against such things there is no law (Galatians 5:22-23 ESV).

For Christ did not please himself, but as it is written, "The reproaches of those who reproached you fell on me." (Romans 15:3 ESV).

Grace to you and peace from God our Father and the Lord Jesus Christ. (Philippians 1:2 ESV).

And the peace of God, which surpasses all understanding, will guard your hearts and your minds in Christ Jesus. (Philippians 4:7).

Review.

We began this study by looking at the command we have from God Himself to rest. If you've ever raised children, you know that sometimes a good sleep can transform the crankiest toddler. We may have gotten more sophisticated in acting out, but we haven't really changed. It's hard to hear God or think clearly if you're exhausted. God tells us to begin with rest and refreshing in Him.

Once refreshed, we need to abide in Christ in order to hear what He has to say and to hear the Holy Spirit direct and guide us.

We've looked at our lives, beginning with our creation and pre-birth, as well as our early years and any trauma experienced. Then we examined the traps behind generational sins, our own sins, lies we may have believed, and how they can open the door to the enemy's attacks. We've looked at word curses from ourselves and others. Go back and review any concepts you may still be unclear on, because a firm understanding of each concept will be helpful grounding as we move into the next section, which will teach you the specific steps necessary to take other through the process of healing prayer.

Regarding healing prayer.

We strongly recommend that you go through your own process of healing prayer before leading others through the steps. Healing prayer can be done on your own, or in a small group — I'd recommend up to three people: a leader who will guide the steps, a prayer support person who will also take notes about key revelations and issues to perhaps address later or continue to pray through, and finally, the one being ministered to through the healing prayer session.

Always begin and end with prayer. If you don't get finished in your first session, be sure to leave the participant in a good place by praying for a fresh filling of the Holy Spirit, whether or not you've finished all the steps. Simply schedule another session. But don't leave them spiritually vulnerable. Remember the lesson of Luke 11:26. You're helping them clean their spiritual house and teaching them how to keep it clean too.

God Moment

Come sit with Me while I soothe your soul and tell you how much I love you and desire your wholeness and complete freedom from all the things that have had you chained to the past. Give Me any lingering sadness or anger. Come under the shelter of My wings and feel My comfort while My anointing flows over you.

Assignment

1. Who would you want to put in the empty chair, and what would you say to them?

2. What are some things that have kept you in chains to your past?

3. Ask the Lord to speak the truth in those memories and write what you hear.

Romans 8:1-2
Galatians 5:22

Final thought:

Whom the Son sets free is free indeed.

Personal Experiences about Healing Prayer

Finding the missing piece.

As a survivor of childhood sexual abuse and an alcoholic, I have gone through lots of traditional therapy. Afterwards, it always felt like there was still a missing piece to my healing. Participating in healing prayer with a trusted guide who was willing to take the time to walk through my past with me, from a traumatic birth to past traumas and poor choices, was the missing piece. Seeing where God was in my story and allowing the Holy Spirit to speak to me and help me hear God more clearly allowed me to unload the weight of my life I had been carrying up to that point. It was time to give it to God. Healing prayer is redeeming and beautiful and intimate and scary, and it gave me the healing I hadn't yet found!

Name withheld

Soul ties can lead to inner vows.

As I have continued down my path of inner healing and transformation, it never occurred to me that I had formed a soul tie with my animals. I just assumed that my deep love for animals was a God-given desire. However, when I looked more deeply at the intense feelings I had around them, I realized that in my childhood, an unhealthy soul tie had been formed. My animals provided me with comfort, presence, and unconditional love.

I had always formed close-knit bonds with my animals, and, for one reason or another, a time invariably came when they would be gone. To my young eyes, pets were so loving and kind that they were safe, much safer than people. So when I lost them, it hurt deeply, and until recently, I think I never really got over those wounds. Now I realize I made an inner vow as a child that when I was grown, I would never get rid of an animal again, for any reason.

Today as I grow in my healing journey, I think even as an adult, I was seeking love, acceptance, presence, and comfort from my animals and had become dependent on them to meet those needs. The fact is, only God can truly meet my needs. And while I still certainly love my animals, I now strive to keep all my relationships — with myself, my animals, humans, and Jesus, in their proper and healthy order, just as He intended.

Name withheld

Seen. Soothed. Healed.

I've always had deeper tremors in the soul than I could quite understand. Under my sanguine nature, a melancholy current always tried to suck me into an ocean of perceived abandonment. A desolate castaway coexisted with my open and curious nature, and even after years of therapy, the shadow lingered.

One sunny morning in her breakfast nook, Linda looked straight at me and said,

"Why don't we try to see what happens when I pray for inner healing for you?"

Sure, why not.

I can't remember how we got there because there was no fanfare or weird incantations happening. Redeemed from New Age witchcraft, I'm very sensitive to any manipulation in the name of Christ, so I need to emphasize how naturally supernatural this was. It was peaceful and conversational, and I felt grounded and present the whole time.

I saw myself as an infant in a dark room. Alone. I can't remember if I was crying or had given up crying for help, only that I had a horrifying awareness that I was alone. Abandoned. And the way I later saw ice flaking off the ice sheets in Greenland, I felt my soul fracture. Maybe that's why I've often felt like I had broken glass in my heart. Splintered.

"Where is Jesus?" Linda asked.

I saw a warming light in the room and felt it wrap my ice-cold soul in an embrace. I felt myself being held against a chest;

He was rocking me soothingly. At first I keep trying to calm my own frantic self, to get a grip, to not be a problem, to not bother Him. I didn't want to wear out His patience. I don't want Him to leave me.

"Don't force it," Linda assures me.

Ahhhh, exhale. Breathe.

We are still in the breakfast nook outside Knoxville, and yet I am entirely present with Jesus in my infant experience. My adult hands wrap around one of Linda's pretty, flowery coffee mugs while I sense the cold, scared places deep inside relax.

We are not forcing anything. Jesus is not in a rush.

Though I can't see His face in this room of my earliest memory, I can feel His warm, rhythmic rocking moving my fractured soul towards wholeness.

Tension leaves, and there's a peaceful stillness inside.

But Linda's wise, blue eyes search my face as she presses in.

"I don't think we're done yet."

Yeah, though I breathe more slowly, there's still that familiar knot somewhere in my abdomen.

"Jesus, please show her what You want her to see."

I'm three years old among several adults in the living room. On the table is a baby carrier with my newborn sister, and I become aware that the ooohing and aaahing is hushing, and they are looking at me. Somehow I know exactly what's expected.

"Look at my little sister. I love her," I lie.

I'm aware that I'm hiding behind the expected words. I'm aware that the overwhelming grief over being displaced by her is inappropriate, that I must swallow any external signs of the devastating loss I'm experiencing, and that from now on, there's no room for me.

My three-year-old self doesn't question the validity of this, nor does she seek comfort or understanding from any of the adults. From then on, she is alone in the world. There is no room for me.

Linda's guiding voice enters the scene:

"Where is Jesus?"

And then I see Him. In this whole room full of people, He only has eyes for me. He sees straight to that place where my soul is hiding behind the polite facade, and His eyes caress me.

"Peekaboo, I see you," He teases, warmly, compassionately. I feel safe. I feel seen.

"What is He telling you?" Linda continues, and somehow He guides the adult me to come and lift up the three-year old little girl. He and I are both holding the scared little kid, not scolding her, but assuring her that we understand. That she's not in trouble and that we will never leave her. There is room for her.

Many years have passed since that sunlit morning in Linda's kitchen, and many opportunities have pricked my old sense of abandonment. But because of her ministry, I've been aware of what it was inside me that was reacting, and I've known how to invite Jesus into caring for the frightened child who may always be with me this side of eternity. But now, I don't abandon her or scold her with religious jargon.

Instead, I join in Jesus' invitation, *"Let the little children come to me, and do not hinder them, for the kingdom of heaven belongs to such as these."* **(Matthew 19:14 NIV)**

Name withheld

A lifetime of abuse, healed.

As a survivor of sexual and ritualistic abuse by my father and his friends from the age of four to seventeen, I didn't understand the impact of such trauma until I started unpacking it in college. I was twenty-one when I first stepped foot into a therapist's office. Needless to say, it took over twenty years for me to speak the words of all the atrocities and walk through the pain and grief each one brought. Was progress made? Absolutely! However, in the depths of my heart, I knew that there was something missing once I left each visit. It took me some time to realize that as much as counseling helped, there were certain situations and flashbacks I couldn't shake no matter how long I talked about them. I needed more than what flesh could give. I needed Jesus.

No one ever wants to go back to painful, humiliating places where shame envelops the soul, but I needed to for so many reasons. I was stuck in a cycle of wrongful thinking, I was struggling with constant nightmares, and I truly thought that what happened to me was my fault in some way. The God I knew and had heard about since I was little would NEVER have allowed this to happen to me … but it happened nevertheless. So my relationship with God was strained. I thought if He loved me enough, He would have saved me. Or worse, if He was there in the midst of the abuse and torture, He must be ashamed of me. I knew that my healing would never truly be lasting unless I invited the Lord into those painful places to see where He was and what He was saying to me in those vulnerable, humiliating, and almost life-threatening experiences.

Healing prayer was hard for me at first because I didn't WANT God to be in those places with me. I didn't want Him watching what was being done to me. As I fought past my pride and self-protection, I found a God totally different than the one I had imagined in my head. He wasn't looking at me in disgust; he was looking at me with heartbreak and compassion. He didn't have His back turned away from me; He was clothing me, placing a blanket over my naked body, or cleaning my wounds. He didn't walk away because He had other priorities; He scooped me up, held me close, and whispered in my ear, "You are mine. No one will ever hurt you again. You are precious to Me. I know what has happened to you, and I can heal your broken heart and show you that I made you for MORE! Hold tightly to me; don't look right or left. You NEVER have to come back here. I am here for YOU."

Instead of focusing on the atrocious acts I went through at a certain point to just work through the pain, healing prayer brought a deeper, lasting healing that could only happen by inviting Jesus into each of those painful places to rescue me. After a few healing prayer sessions, I felt such peace and freedom … two basic needs anyone longs for, especially me since they were purposely withheld from me at such an early age. More than that, my thinking began to change, my nightmares were less frequent, I was able to go off my sleeping and PTSD medication, I no longer carry around the shame I wore as a shield, and it brought comfort to all those parts of me who longed to be someone's little girl. Healing prayer brought such freedom that I found counseling wasn't a necessity anymore.

When those painful reminders still pop up, healing prayer has given me the tools to bring Jesus into those places to set me free again … and again … however long it takes. As scripture says, *if God is truly for me, who can be against me?* Now I know! I am no longer a victim but a victor, and I am precious in His sight.

Name withheld

Transformed life and family after abortion, drugs.

One of the most traumatic events in my life was a choice to abort a child when I was around 19 years old. I didn't want to abort, however, I was in a toxic relationship, and I was told if I did not abort the baby, this man would utilize his family and resources and take the baby away, and I would never see it again. Emotionally and physically exhausted, I finally agreed. The day of the abortion felt like part of my soul died. I had a very hard time looking myself in the mirror and was not sure how God could ever forgive me when I could not even forgive myself. The pain caused me to run from that relationship and delve deep into drug addiction with crystal meth. Then began a very bad 7-year addiction. I was not merely a recreational drug user — it became a lifestyle for me and nearly destroyed my life. I ruined relationships and lost everything important to me. Eventually, in the middle of my addiction, I found myself pregnant after only knowing the father a few short months. I continued to use throughout my pregnancy just avoiding the fact that I was pregnant. I knew I could not have an abortion, though many of my friends were pushing it. Believe it or not, the father of this baby was praying and hoping I would have the baby.

Eventually I went to the doctor at 18 weeks along. It was there that I poured my heart out to the doctor and told him everything. He ordered an ultra sound that day. I was sure I had hurt this baby with my drug use. They put the Doppler on my belly and lifted it quickly. The technician asked me, "Did you know?" and I replied, "Know what?" The technician looked at me and said, "That you're having two!" As she put the Doppler back on my belly, she moved it quickly and said "Girl – Girl, two girls!" It was at that moment, for the first time in my life that I felt the presence of God. Everything in the room disappeared, and I heard Him tell my heart that He trusted me with life. Not only did He trust me, He gave me back double what I stole from Him. My journey of healing had begun. When I was full term, I had to be induced, but by the grace of God, the babies were born happy and healthy at 7 pounds each. I tried desperately to just get healthy, though I did not know how. I battled my addiction for two more years before getting real help. I finally walked into a Teen Challenge center for women and children on 08/25/2004. My girls joined me three weeks later, and I graduated on October 05, 2005. It was that day that I told the father of my babies to choose life so that his descendants may live. He did — we healed quite a bit and ended up married with one more child born in 2008.

Although I had experienced quite a bit of faith-based healing starting in 2004, I still struggled with deep trauma I could not recognize. When my son was learning to swim, I would find myself extremely panicky and frozen in fear. It was a fear response that was beyond what the circumstances called for. I reached out to a friend who helped women walk through healing prayer. I explained to her what I was dealing with, and she offered to take it to the Lord with me. Upon sitting quietly with the Lord, allowing my friend to help guide me, and prompting certain questions to my heart and the Lord, we invited the Holy Spirit in for help. The Holy Spirit identified that the enemy had used my abortion to bury lies within that trauma, which would impact the way I lived. The biggest lie revealed that day was that because of my abortion I was due retribution from the Lord, and I should be on guard as He could take my son, or any of my children, at any minute. It caused me to live in extreme fear, to be a "helicopter parent," and react in ways that were unhealthy. Holy Spirit then spoke the healing balm of truth to my heart which brought great peace and healing to that area. I wholeheartedly trust that my children are actually the Lord's first before they are mine. I know He has fully forgiven me for the loss of my first child. I also believe He cares about my children and will keep them safe. I know that, should hard experiences happen, He will not leave me or my children but will be there next to us.

Being able to go back to the pool for the first time after that session was nothing short of amazing. I sat in peace and watched while my son took swimming lessons from his swim coach. I saw the situation through a different filter, the filter of a healed heart.

I still keep watch since the enemy likes to use my trauma to continue to hurt me in different ways. But I now know exactly how to go to the Lord, work through identifying the lies of the enemy, and how to replace those lies with the Truth of God.

Name withheld

Section Two

ACTION SECTION
STEPS TO HEALING PRAYER
FOR YOURSELF AND OTHERS

The Lord is near to the brokenhearted and saves the crushed in spirit. (Psalm 34:18 ESV)

A joyful heart is good medicine, but a crushed spirit dries up the bones. (Proverbs 17:22 ESV)

A man without self-control is like a city broken into and left without walls. (Proverbs 25:28 ESV)

PRE-SESSION NOTES & INSTRUCTIONS

Prepare yourself

- Be confident you have authority over the enemy.
- Read Isaiah 61:1-4 (NKJV):
  "The Spirit of the Lord God is upon Me, Because the Lord has anointed Me to preach good tidings to the poor; He has sent Me to heal the brokenhearted, To proclaim liberty to the captives, And the opening of the prison to those who are bound; To proclaim the acceptable year of the Lord, And the day of vengeance of our God; To comfort all who mourn, To console those who mourn in Zion, To give them beauty for ashes, The oil of joy for mourning, The garment of praise for the spirit of heaviness; That they may be called trees of righteousness, The planting of the Lord, that He may be glorified." And they shall rebuild the old ruins, They shall raise up the former desolations, And they shall repair the ruined cities, The desolations of many generations.
- Remember to always begin with prayer. Invite the Holy Spirit to come and lead during this time. Thank Jesus for the authority (in Luke 9 and 2 Corinthians 10) He has given to us to bring freedom to the captives. Pray for peace and comfort for yourself and all participants, praying that they would be able to hear the voice of the Holy Spirit. This is the key to healing prayer — to hear the voice of the Lord.

He called the twelve together and gave them power and authority over all demons and to cure diseases. (Luke 9:1 ESV)

For even if I boast a little too much of our authority, which the Lord gave for building you up and not for destroying you, I will not be ashamed. (2 Corinthians 10:8 ESV)

- REMEMBER: Before going through the steps with others, be sure you've first gone through the steps yourself, either alone or with someone else.

GETTING STARTED

Beginning session prayer: *"Lord, I ask You to station warring angels about this room and property. I ask that they would hold back any forces of darkness that would try to interfere with this ministry. I ask that You protect those of us in this room and our families from any attack of the enemy as a result of this ministry time. Amen."*

If working with someone else, have them close their eyes and lead them in repeating the following prayer out loud. Otherwise, read the prayer yourself out loud.

Prayer: *"Lord Jesus, I thank you for the authority you have delegated to us against the enemy, especially to bring freedom to those held captive. I pray for peace and comfort for* ____________________ *and that he/she would be active and responsive during this time. Holy Spirit, we invite you to come and lead us in how to pray and what to pray. I speak to any evil spirits that would try to linger in this place, and I say in the name of Jesus, you will not remain here or follow anyone when they leave. You must leave this property, and you are forbidden to go to any of our family members. Amen."*

There's not always time to go through all the steps advised here in a single healing prayer session. No matter where you stop for the day, at the end of the prayer session, always cover step twelve and give the participant scripture verses that are applicable to their needs. The word of God is always the most effective weapon we have against the enemy.

GETTING STARTED

STEP ONE

Begin at the beginning: conception.[1]

INSTRUCTION: Read the following scriptures aloud:

"Before I formed you in the womb I knew you,
and before you were born I consecrated you;
I appointed you a prophet to the nations." **(Jeremiah 1:5 ESV)**

You know when I sit down and when I rise up;
you discern my thoughts from afar. **(Psalm 139:2 ESV)**

To stay focused, it helps to keep your eyes closed.

Picture the hands of God, present at your own conception, holding an egg in one hand and a sperm in the other. God specifically chose that egg and that sperm to create you. Picture His hands coming together to form you. Then, in your own words, (out loud) bless the act of your conception.

Prayer: *In Jesus's name, I bless the act of my conception with (list the things you would like to have seen your life blessed with.)*

1 For background on this step, see lesson 3 beginning on page 29.

STEP TWO
Return to the beginning, blessing each trimester.[1]

Instruction: While in the womb, if any negative emotions surface, such as fear or anxiety, it has nothing to do with the baby. Hence, it's not the baby's fault. Realize these feelings are coming from whatever the mother was feeling or experiencing at the time. It's interesting that many of these feelings that surface in the womb seem to follow a person throughout life.

Write down any feelings that come up during each trimester of gestation. Don't be concerned if no feelings surface during the first trimester.

First trimester ______________________________

Second trimester ____________________________

Third trimester ______________________________

When it's time to be born, what are the feelings that surface about being born?

____

Next, see the adult version of yourself as you are now standing outside the womb watching as you are being born.

Picture Jesus receiving the baby and handing it to the adult version of yourself as you stand there with Him. (Scripture says that He is always with us, Matthew 28:20.)

Bless your birth by praying:

1 For background on this step, see lesson 3 beginning on page 29.

Prayer: *"Lord, in the name of Jesus, I bless my birth with excitement and joy and peace. I bless this baby's life with … (personalize this; it will usually be the opposite of the curses revealed earlier) and I ask that these blessings be handed down a thousand generations."* **(Exodus 20:6)**

STEP THREE
Break the power of generational sins and curses.[1]

Instruction: Ask the Lord to reveal the generational sins and curses in the family line. Remember, sin is defined as deliberate disobedience to God's word. Demonic familial spirits that attached to the sin continue through the family line to attack generations. The prayer below is helpful. Write down the list of sins, curses, or familial spirits revealed by Holy Spirit.

What comes to mind, revealed by the Spirit, may be things you were previously unaware of. You may never have participated in the sins and curses mentioned. It could be things like adultery, divorce, incest, perversion, addictions, etc.

Now, repent on behalf of your ancestors and forgive them.

Many times there is also a need to repent for blaming the Lord for allowing this to happen. And of course, if you, too, have committed the same sins, there is a need for you to confess, repent, and also forgive yourself.

Prayer: *"Holy Spirit, I give you permission to reveal any sins and resulting curses in my bloodline. (Wait and listen for the Holy Spirit to make the revelations. List them and then continue.) Lord, I repent on behalf of my ancestors for the sins of ____, _____, _____, (etc.), I confess and repent of my own sins that would open doors for any familial spirits to attack my children, and I ask your forgiveness. I forgive myself as I also choose to forgive those in my ancestral line that are responsible for these demonic attachments. In the name of Jesus, I cancel these demonic assignments against myself and my children as a result of these sins. Amen."*

1 For background on this step, see lesson 4 beginning on page 37.

Picture the cross of Jesus between the baby in the womb and any evil spirits that would try to attach to curses in the family line. Ask the Lord to protect this baby from this day forward.

Remember that healing prayer is not just a one-time event. The Holy Spirit will continue to reveal things to you in your life or your family line that you need to confess, repent, forgive, and replace with blessings.

STEP FOUR Healing of past traumatic and painful memories — Theophostic.[1]

Instruction: It's important to continue to keep your eyes closed as much as possible; it helps stay focused. Also write down each memory (or have someone present do so).

Ask the Holy Spirit to reveal any traumatic or painful events during your former years, beginning from birth to present time.

Wait for the Holy Spirit to bring memories to mind. Take your time as you work through your life. Write down what the Lord brings up as significant painful events.

Painful, traumatic memories might be physical, emotional, or sexual abuse, a death, accident, divorce, etc. As emotions surface that are connected to these memories such as guilt, fear, anger, sadness, shame, etc., make a side note to address these by name when it's time at the end to break off strongholds in the next step (page 108).

When negative emotions surface, pray aloud, asking the True Lord Jesus to show where He is in the memory. Don't guide the person.

There is always a lie attached to the trauma, so when the lie is revealed, ask Jesus to speak the truth. Write down what Jesus says and what you see Him doing. (When we ask the True Lord Jesus to come, there is almost never a counterfeit spirit that shows up. A good way to be sure is that what is heard is kind, affirming, encouraging, etc.)

1 For background on this step, see lessons 4 and 8 beginning on pages 37 and 73, respectively..

There is always a lie you have believed attached to the memory, typically along the lines of, *"it's my fault; if I tell, I will die or someone close to me will die; there must be something wrong with me; I'm a bad person; nobody cares; nobody loves me; if people find out they won't like me; I didn't get it right,"* etc.

Write down the lies attached to the trauma, as well as what Jesus said about it.

Example: *You, or whomever you might be ministering to, are back in a memory of abuse and no one is there to help. What feelings are surfacing?*

Now look around the room to see where Jesus is in the memory. If He isn't visible, is there are a sense of His presence? Even if you can't see Him, you can still listen for Him to speak.

This is important because when the Lord speaks truth, it breaks the power of the lie.

Ask the True Lord Jesus to allow you to hear Him speak truth, or allow you to see Him doing something. If trauma is involved, the details don't have to be recorded.

Now go from birth throughout your life by asking for significant memories and trauma experienced during each of these time periods. Invite the Lord into the memories and journal what you hear and/or what you see Him doing. To experience freedom, it's important to forgive whoever hurt you or caused you to be hurt in any way.

- Toddler years, from birth to age three.

- Preschool, ages 4-6.

- Elementary school years, ages 7-10.

- Middle school years, ages 11-13

- High school years ages, 14-18.

- College and young adult years.

- Adulthood to present time.

If you have trouble with any part of this step, read over the Troubleshooting advice on page 108 and try again.

Troubleshooting

When asked to picture a memory or anything else, if you see only darkness, there is probably a spirit blocking the ministry of the Holy Spirit, or you have unforgiveness, which keeps you from seeing, sensing, and feeling the memory. Ask who you need to forgive, and do so. Also, if this happens, tell the enemy that he has to go and to stop interfering with the ministry.

> IMPORTANT: ***You must forgive those who hurt you, and yourself, as well as stop blaming God for allowing it. Just as we have anger and unforgiveness toward people, we can feel those things against God, too.***

Sometimes you are able to "see" better after forgiving and surrendering your will.

It's the inner child, the one who suffered the trauma, who keeps reminding you of the pain and making accusations against you. The unforgiveness of the inner child will keep the guilt and pain coming back up as he/she continues to accuse the adult you've become. Sometimes it is helpful as an adult to go to the inner child in the memory and comfort them.

Dr. Clark Stevens, a clinical psychologist in Knoxville, TN, suggested another method that is helpful in situations like this: have the adult who is receiving ministry to visualize facing the perpetrator while the inner child is behind their back, as if the adult is protecting the inner child during the confrontation. Then the adult can tell the perpetrator exactly what they think of them and inform them that now they are protecting this child and the perpetrator can no longer hurt them.

Example: *One woman who had been sexually abused as a child buried the memories deeply (psychologists call this "disassociation".) She didn't remember the abuse until age 17 when the memories returned. After realizing the extent of her abuse, she started living a life of addiction and promiscuity in an attempt to numb her pain. After doing this for 30 years, she began a road of sobriety and healing. During one of several healing prayer sessions, she pictured herself as the little girl who had been abused. She was then instructed, as that child, to stand behind her adult self and face the perpetrator. She was finally able to confront the perpetrator and say all the things the little girl (her inner child) was never able to say. After this exercise, she was then able to forgive the perpetrator, both as the little girl and her adult self. Later she commented about even being able to breathe better and how much freedom she received after that exercise.*

Evil doesn't make sense. It comes down to faith in God's character and goodness, and your willingness to forgive and stop blaming — even God for allowing it. Forgiving the perpetrator. Forgiving yourself. Letting go of guilt and reactions.

If you're reluctant to release strongholds such as shame, hatred, unforgiveness, etc., it's often because you are unsure of who you'll be without the strongholds. The answer is wonderful: You'll be who God designed you to be!

STEP FIVE

Deliverance from demonic attachments.[1]

Stronghold Groupings

Fear

Fear will have attached to it spirits of Inferiority, Insecurity, Worry, Anxiety, Panic, Phobias, Perfectionism, Fear of failure, Tormenting spirits, and Night terrors.

Shame

Shame is usually accompanied by Guilt, Deception, Lying spirits, and Self-hatred, as well as Blame, Condemnation, Embarrassment, and Stupidity.

Death

Death is usually accompanied by Suicide, Infirmity, Death Wish, and anything that attacks the body, such as Addictions: drugs, nicotine, alcoholism, as well as Anorexia, Bulimia and Abortion. Also, Sickness, Constant Pain, Miscarriage, Hate, and Starvation.

Pride

Pride is usually accompanied by Fear, Worry, Anxiety, Obsessive-Compulsive (OCD) behavior, Perfectionism, and Tormenting spirits. Also, Over-performance, Manipulation, Lying, Mocking, and Sarcasm.

Rejection

Rejection will typically also have spirits of Insecurity, Abandonment and Neglect or Self-hatred, Addictive behavior, Compulsions, Withdrawal, Loneliness, Neglect, and Jealousy. Also Isolation and Self-destruction.

1 For background on this step, see lesson 8 beginning on page 73.

Hate

Hate will include Self-hatred, Anger, Cutting, Piercing, Excessive tattooing, and Self-punishment.

Anger

Anger will usually have spirits of Bitterness, Resentment, Depression, and sometimes Rage attached, as well as Unforgiveness and Revenge.

Lust

Lust will typically include spirits of Pornography, Fantasy, Adultery, Perversion, Shame, Homosexuality, Incest, Seduction, and Masturbation.

Heaviness

Heaviness usually opens the door to spirits of Depression, Despair, Self-pity, Suicidal thoughts, Condemnation, Sadness, Grieving, and Mourning.

Divination

Divination will have spirits of Witchcraft and Control along with Confusion, Fatigue, Guilt, Confliction, Familiar Spirits, Manipulation, Tarot cards, Palm reading, and Curses. (See 1 Samuel)

Occult

Occult Spirits of Deception include New Age, Necromancy, Psychic readings, Religious spirits, Freemasonry, Scientology, Mormonism, Islam, and Buddhism, as well as others, such as Anti-Christ spirits and Familiar spirits.

Most of the time, evil spirits attached to traumatic memories continue to harass the person. To help the process of being free, it's useful to know some issues that typically appear together. Some groupings you might expect, others may be a little surprising. For instance, read through the groupings listed above.

Instruction: First, ask Jesus to have the angels prepare boxes, one for each grouping, into which the strongholds will be placed. These boxes will be at the feet of Jesus.

Start with the first box that has Fear written on it. Command the stronghold, along with all the spirits that accompany it, to go into the box. Say, for example:

Prayer: *"In the name of Jesus, I command the spirit of Fear to go into the box at the feet of Jesus. I bind the spirit of Worry, Anxiety, Perfectionism, and any spirit associated with the spirit of Fear and command you to go into the box too. I cancel every demonic assignment. You have no legal right to harass me (her/him if praying for someone else) anymore."*

Check to see if anything is left outside the box. For example, when dealing with the stronghold of Fear, if the spirit of perfectionism is left outside the box, command it to go in. If there's resistance, ask the Lord why it has not gone into the box. Once the resistance is cleared, again, command it to go into the box. Usually, it will be related to unforgiveness of someone, blaming God, or agreement with the spirit. This can result in a reluctance to confess, repent, and forgive. After the resistance has cleared, command the spirit to go into the box. Ask Jesus to lock and dispose of the box in any way He sees fit. If the box is still there, ask the Lord why. Make sure you are not holding onto anything, such as unforgiveness, that gives legal rights to the enemy.

Repeat this prayer for each of the major stronghold groupings listed. Remember, confession, repentance, and forgiveness cancel the enemy's legal right to accuse.

Finally, ask the Lord to release any spiritual gifts that have been stagnant. Speak blessings of love, joy, peace, and other fruits of the Spirit.

It's important to begin the process of correcting wrong beliefs, attitudes, and reactions. Old habits can now be broken, but counseling may be needed as a follow up in order to do that. Do not see yourself as a victim but rather as a victor.

Pray for an infilling of the Holy Spirit now if you don't cover all the steps (Galatians 5:22). This is very important. If you have more time, you can also cover this at the end, but be sure to do this before the session ends.

Prayer: *"Father, in the name of Jesus, I ask for a fresh infilling of the Holy Spirit. I ask you to fill all the places swept clean with all the fruit of the Spirit: love, peace, joy, faith, goodness, gentleness, patience, kindness, and self-control. I release any spiritual gifts that have been stagnant in my life and ministry as a result of believing lies. Amen."*

STEP SIX
Breaking unholy yokes, ungodly soul ties.[1]

Instruction: Repent of any ungodly relationships or words shared with others. This can be sexual or emotional; it can also involve friends whose main tie was through gossip or control; it can involve parents, children, other relatives, or even a pet. It could be a blood covenant, that is, cutting oneself to make a vow.

An unholy soul tie could be someone you have had a co-dependent relationship with where one person is enabling the other.

Keep in mind, you may need to come against any familiar spirits attached that connected you to the person with whom you or they had the soul tie. The old saying, "birds of a feather flock together," would come from this kind of attachment. Familiar spirits would be things like perversions, insecurities, suspicion, and critical or gossipy spirits — any negative common ground.

When praying to break the ties, you can give first names only. If some names have been forgotten, ask the Lord to hang pictures of their faces on a wall in a hallway. As you walk down the hallway and look at the pictures, you can confess, repent, and forgive each one in turn. Sometimes after this is done, the pictures disappear off the wall.

Prayer: *"In the name of Jesus, I repent of and renounce all sinful and unholy acts and break a soul tie with ____________. Lord, I ask you now to break any and all ungodly soul ties and demonic*

---

1 For background on this step, see lesson 5 beginning on page 49.

attachments. In the name of Jesus, I command all familiar spirits and any other spirits attached to these ties to leave me and go where Jesus sends you. Lord, I thank you for delivering me. Amen."

Remember to forgive the person with whom the soul ties were broken. Ask the Lord to restore torn and broken places in the soul that are a result of these unhealthy relationships. This is when someone was given, or allowed to take, some part of the soul that wasn't that person's to have.

Prayer: *"I ask you, Father, in the name of Jesus, to bring back any broken and torn places in my heart and soul as a result of these relationships. I repent of allowing someone else to take from me what wasn't his or hers to have. I ask that you would completely restore my soul. I let go of anything I've held onto regarding the relationship. I ask you to forgive me as I forgive them. I forgive myself for participating in the sin. I release them to you to be all you created them to be. Amen."*

- Ask the Lord what the torn and broken places are.
- Release your feelings of blame if you have blamed God for allowing it.
- Ask the Lord if there was any childhood sexual abuse that you don't remember.

It might be necessary to pray to sever ties with locations.

Prayer: *"Dear Lord Jesus Christ, I bring into the light the locations of ________________, where I participated in the sinful acts of ______________. I repent for and renounce all these unholy acts that I participated in or that were forced upon me at these locations as well as the accompanying objects of* (if applicable) ________________, (These could be paraphernalia, clothes, gifts, mementos, etc.)

Prayer: *"I now ask you, Lord, to sever any and all unholy ties, alliances, or demonic attachments I have with these locations or objects. I command all demonic spirits that have gained access to me, my body, soul, or spirit as a result of these unholy acts at these locations or with these objects, to leave me now and never return and go to the place where Jesus Christ sends you.*

"I now ask you, Lord, to bring back any part of me that has been held captive as a result of these unholy acts done at these locations or with these objects. Please completely restore my soul and heal my memories regarding these places and things. Please make my heart whole and wholly yours. I now release anything regarding those locations or objects that I have held onto. I take back all ground I wrongfully surrendered at those places or to those things, and I ask you to heal and bless that land for Kingdom purposes. Amen."

STEP SEVEN
Renounce and repent of inner vows, and replace them with Godly purposes.[1]

Renounce and repent of inner vows and replace them with Godly purposes. These are thing like, *I will never do a certain thing or be a certain way or allow someone to do or be to me certain things.*

INSTRUCTION: Name the vows that you have made as the Lord reveals them and write down the list.

____

____

Ask God what His will and purposes are instead and write these down also.

____

____

Confess and ask forgiveness for making these vows, and also forgive anyone else who was involved.

Also repent of any judgmental attitudes that may have formed toward anyone that contributed to you forming an inner vow.

Prayer: *"Father, in the name of Jesus, I confess and repent of making the inner vow of ____________ and depending on myself rather than relying on You. Instead of doing this in my own strength, I ask You to help me not to (be, do) ____________________. Thank You for Your grace and mercy. I repent of any judgmental*

1 For background on this step, see lesson 6 beginning on page 59.

attitudes I have held against those who contributed to my making these vows. I ask Your forgiveness, and I forgive those who contributed to my making the vows. Amen."

STEP EIGHT
Cancel word curses.[1]

Word curses are negative declarations we have said about ourselves or things others have said to or about us that we've taken to heart in a hurtful way. Any labels or names we have put on ourselves or others have spoken about us become curses when we come into agreement with the negative words or labels. They cause negative beliefs about oneself.

> **INSTRUCTION:** Ask the Lord to bring to mind any word curses spoken over you during your lifetime. Following the structure of confession, repentance, and forgiveness, we need to forgive the people involved (even if it's you), bless them, and cancel any effects experienced as a result of these curses in the name of Jesus. Ask Jesus how He blesses you instead.

Prayer: *"Lord, I confess and repent of the word curses I have spoken over and about myself. I ask Your forgiveness, and I forgive those who have spoken these words over me as well. I ask You to speak to me about who You say I am and break the power of these words over my mind and body. Thank you, Lord, for showing me the truth. Amen."*

1 For background on this step, see lesson 7 beginning on page 67.

STEP NINE
Replace negative beliefs with God's promises.[1]

Instruction: Negative beliefs are false beliefs or conclusions we believe about God, a situation, expectations, or ourselves about our circumstances. They are contrary to God's promises about who we are.

Pray the prayer below, confessing any negative beliefs (lies) held about yourself or God. Ask the Lord to reveal what the lies are, make a list, and then pray.

Write down the list as each one comes to mind.

Prayer: *"Lord, I confess and repent for believing the lie of ______________________________________. I repent for not believing or even asking You what You say about me instead. I ask You to forgive me, and I forgive anyone who has contributed to my believing these lies. Amen."*

Instruction: Ask God what His promises are instead. Sometimes it is helpful to write out the lies that have been believed and burn them.

Remember — Safety first!

1 For background on this step, see lesson 7 beginning on page 67.

STEP TEN
Theo therapy — empty chair.[1]

Instruction: Use the Theo Therapy empty chair technique during your healing prayer session; imagine the person who hurt you is sitting across from you in a chair used for this purpose. Then, verbalize all your feelings of anger, hatred, resentment, hurt, loss, etc., toward the person. When you've finished getting all the feelings out and expressed, forgive the offending person, forgive yourself for the feelings, and God for allowing it. Lastly, release the person who wounded you to the Lord.

Prayer: *"Father, in the name of Jesus, I confess and repent of unforgiveness toward ______________. I forgive them now and release them to You. Thank You for Your grace and mercy. Amen."*

1 For background on this step, see lesson 8 beginning on page 73.

STEP ELEVEN
Deal with any lingering anger or sadness.[1]

Instruction: If there are still feelings of either anger or sadness, tell Jesus about it. After you've told Him about it, be willing to let it go. Ask Jesus to take the anger or sadness upon Himself.

1 For background on this step, see lesson 8 beginning on page 73.

STEP TWELVE
Blessing, cleansing, protection, and infilling prayer.[1]

Instruction: Pray to receive a fresh infilling of the Holy Spirit, and ask the Holy Spirit to seal the work He has done. Cast any lingering spirits out of the room and off the property. Forbid them from going to any other family member or home.

Prayer: *"Father, in the name of Jesus, I ask for a fresh infilling of the Holy Spirit. I ask you to fill all the places swept clean with all the fruit of the Spirit: love, peace, joy, faith, goodness, gentleness, patience, kindness, and self-control. I release any spiritual gifts that have been stagnant in my life and ministry as a result of believing lies. Amen."*

Prayer: *"Lord, in the name of Jesus, I ask that you would seal the work you have done. I command any lingering spirits to leave this property, and I say that, in the Name of Jesus, you will not try to attach yourself to any other family member. And Father, I ask that you bless each one here today through your Holy Spirit in Jesus' Name I pray. Amen."*

Then, pray these scriptures out loud for blessings so you hear them and they get down into your spirit:

Do not be anxious about anything, but in everything by prayer and supplication with thanksgiving let your requests be made known to God. And the peace of God, which surpasses all understanding, will guard your hearts and your minds in Christ Jesus. Finally, brothers, whatever is true, whatever is honorable, whatever is just, whatever is pure, whatever is

1 For background on this step, see lesson 8 beginning on page 73.

lovely, whatever is commendable, if there is any excellence, if there is anything worthy of praise, think about these things. (Philippians 4:6-8 ESV)

Rejoice in the Lord always, I will say it again: Rejoice. (Philippians 4:4)

So then, brothers, we are debtors, not to the flesh, to live according to the flesh (Romans 8:12 ESV).

For freedom Christ has set us free; stand firm therefore, and do not submit again to a yoke of slavery. (Galatians 5:1 ESV).

As noted earlier:

If you run short of time, make sure you cover this step, no matter where you need to end the prayer work.

Scriptures for blessing:

There is therefore now no condemnation for those who are in Christ Jesus. For the law of the Spirit of life has set you free in Christ Jesus from the law of sin and death.

(Romans 8:1-2 ESV)

But the fruit of the Spirit is love, joy, peace, patience, kindness, goodness, faithfulness, gentleness, self-control; against such things there is no law.

(Galatians 5:22-23 ESV)

For Christ did not please himself, but as it is written, "The reproaches of those who reproached you fell on me."

(Romans 15:3 ESV)

Grace to you and peace from God our Father and the Lord Jesus Christ.

(Philippians 1:2 ESV)

And the peace of God, which surpasses all understanding, will guard your hearts and your minds in Christ Jesus.

(Philippians 4:7)

IMPORTANT: ***You must forgive those who hurt you, forgive yourself, and forgive God for allowing it. Just as we have anger and unforgiveness toward people, we can feel those things against God, too.***

Journal:

Summary of Steps and Associated Prayers

1. Begin at the beginning by praying, *"Lord, I bless the act of my conception."*
2. Break the power of generational sins and curses by praying, *"Holy Spirit, I give you permission to reveal any sins and curses in my bloodline."* Then, name what comes to mind, repent, and forgive. Repent on behalf of your ancestors.
3. Return to the beginning, asking for any emotions felt during each trimester. Then, bless each month in the womb, ending with this prayer: *"Lord, in the name of Jesus, I bless my birth with excitement and joy and peace. I bless this baby's life with* ... (it will usually be the opposite of the curses revealed in Step 2), *and I ask that these blessings be handed down a thousand generations."*
4. Heal past traumatic and painful memories.
5. Deliverance from demonic attachments — like Shame, Guilt, Deception, Lying, etc. — by prayer.
6. Break unholy yokes or soul ties.
7. Renounce and repent of inner vows and replace them with Godly purposes.
8. Cancel word curses.
9. Renounce and replace negative beliefs with God's promises.
10. Theo therapy – empty chair.
11. Deal with any lingering anger or sadness.

    For yourself or any participant of healing prayer, you may want to consider following up with a professional Christian counselor to continue the healing process.

12. Blessing, cleansing, protection, and infilling prayer.

Journal:

APPENDIX

Recommended reading for further study

Search for Significance, by Robert McGee

Pain and Pretending, by Rich Buhler

Healing for Damaged Emotions Workbook, by David Seamans

Two Hours to Freedom, by Dr. Charles Kraft

Prayers that Heal the Heart, by Mark Virkler

Stone by Stone, by Jasona Brown

Hiding from Love, by Dr. John Townsend

Hearing the Voice of God, by Mark Virkler

The Secret Life of the Unborn Child, by Thomas Verney

The Healing Light (Christ), by Agnes Sanford

Restoring the Christian Soul through Healing Prayer, by Leanne Payne

You Can Be Emotionally Free, by Rita Bennett

Transforming the Inner Man, by John Loren Sandford & Paula Sandford

The Practice of Healing Prayer, A How-to Guide for Catholics, by Francis MacNutt, Ph.D., founder of Christian Healing Ministries

Healing Prayer from the Effects of Trauma with thanks and credit to Deeper Still

Dear Father, Son & Holy Spirit,

I come before you today and come boldly before your throne of grace. I completely submit to your love, power, and wisdom as I pray for complete healing from the effects of trauma in my body, soul, and spirit. I seek to appropriate the all-encompassing provision of the atoning grace of my Lord and Savior, Jesus Christ. I thank you, Jesus, that by your stripes, I am healed.

In the powerful name of Jesus Christ, I call my spirit to attention, and I call my soul and body to be in submission to my spirit as it is in submission to the Holy Spirit of God. I agree for my body and soul to come into alignment with the perfect word and will of God. I now take authority over any and all terrestrial (earth bound) demonic spirits that would seek to interfere with my healing intervention. In the powerful name of Jesus Christ and by His blood, I bind and gag these demonic spirits.

In the name of Jesus Christ, I command that any and all negative effects from the traumas I've endured come out of my body and my whole being even down to the cellular level. I specifically call out the incidents I've endured of: __________________ (identify things such as: physical, emotional, spiritual, and sexual abuse and perversions, rape, homosexuality, divorce, deaths, significant losses, adoption, accidents, injuries, surgeries, abortion, frequent moves, rejections, abandonment, major illnesses, attempted suicide, ritual abuse, etc. Take a few minutes to allow the Holy Spirit to bring these events to your conscious memory and speak them out.)

I ask you Lord to deliver and heal my body and soul from these events. I ask you, Lord, to bless my lymphatic system and other bodily systems to safely remove all wastes, toxins, poisons, chemicals, stress hormones, excessive enzymes or any other product or by-product from these traumas to my body and soul. I also call out all negative effects of anesthetics or any drugs that were addictive or caused harmful side effects. I command all these negative effects to be neutralized and healed and that all traces of these destructive substances come out of my body and soul without harm or injury in the name of Jesus.

I now command all long and short-term effects of trauma: stress, tension, worry, anxiety, fear, grief, and wounding to come out as well as all memories of abuse, defiling touch, beatings, bruises, harsh words, words of limitation or curses spoken over me by significant authorities and relationships, or as a result of generational iniquity. I also command out of my body and soul the memory of all smells, feelings, tastes, sounds, vibrations, and touch connected to those events. I ask you, Lord, to heal, re-create and redeem my genetic DNA according to your design and purposes.

Father God, would you also dismantle all automatic human responses that were initiated as a result of these traumas, such as right responses, triggers, fears, and phobias. Lord, would you rebuild, re-establish, and re-create any electrical or chemical connections that were broken or improperly re-connected as a result of these traumas so I can function and respond normally in the presence of stimuli.

I now ask you, Father God, to disconnect, deliver, and shield me from any and all principalities, authorities, powers, dominions, thrones, world forces of darkness, spiritual forces of wickedness in heavenly places, and ungodly celestial beings that have gained access to me through these traumatic events with the intent of bringing me ongoing torment, affliction, or bondage. I declare that Jesus Christ has put all these enemies under His feet and that, because I am in Christ, I am now seated with Him in heavenly places, and He has put all these enemies in subjection, under His feet.

I also ask you, Father God, that You shut down all pathways, portals, marks, markers, or any other means of access or connectivity that these entities would have to communicate, influence, or track me physically or spiritually. I thank you that on whatever lands or nations my feet step, I am under the shadow of the Almighty, covered by His pinions and delivered from the deadly pestilence.

In the name of Jesus, and by the authority of His blood, I also cancel all assignments or curses of familiar spirits made against me as a result of these traumatic events. And, I ask you, Father God, who alone sits as Judge in the court of heaven, that You issue a cease and desist order to all tormenting spirits and spiritual entities.

Next, I ask you, Father God, in the name of your son Jesus Christ, that if any portion of my being has been delayed, trapped, captured or imprisoned in another time, space, dimension or place as a result of these traumas that you would cause those parts of my soul to be released, rejoined, and reunified with my core being in this current time, space, and dimension. I also ask that you would release healing and deliverance through each age and stage of my entire life from when you first knew me and said, "Yes," to my existence up until this present time. I ask you to mature each re-integrated portion of my being into my current age.

Now, Lord, would you re-establish the connection between the right and left hemispheres of my brain and synchronize the necessary memories that need to be retrieved for complete healing.

Father God, I ask you to re-establish appropriate sleep patterns for me and to give me sweet, undisturbed, rejuvenating, and regenerative sleep. Give me Godly dreams and visions in the night season. When I go to sleep at night and entrust myself to your keeping, will you watch over my body, soul, and spirit and allow me to receive everything I need for the day ahead.

Thank you, Father, Son, and Holy Spirit. Lastly, I ask you to cover and heal any other area of my life that is hidden or blocked from my conscience. I give you all the glory for this finished work. Amen!

Masonry Release

(Also includes prayers of release from many other related occult organizations)

If you or someone you love is a descendant of a Mason, CHM recommends that you pray through the following prayers from your heart. Please read it through first so you know what is involved. It is best to pray aloud with a Christian witness or counselor present.

Father God, Creator of heaven and earth, I come to You in the Name of Jesus Christ, Your Son. I come as a sinner seeking forgiveness and cleansing from all sins committed against You. I honor my earthly father and mother and all of my ancestors of flesh and blood, and my parents and/or ancestors of the spirit by adoption, and my god-parents, but I utterly turn away from and renounce all their sins. I forgive my ancestors for the effects of their sins on me and my children. I confess and renounce all of my own sins. I renounce and rebuke Satan and every spiritual power of his affecting me and my family.

I renounce and forsake all involvement in Freemasonry or any other lodge or craft by my ancestors and myself. I renounce witchcraft, the principal spirit behind Freemasonry, and I renounce Baphomet, the Spirit of Antichrist, and the curse of the Luciferian doctrine. I renounce the idolatry, blasphemy, secrecy, and deception of Masonry at every level. I specifically renounce the insecurity, the love of position and power, the love of money, avarice or greed, and the pride which would have led my ancestors into Masonry. I renounce all the fears which held them in Masonry, especially the fears of death, fears of men, and fears of trusting, in the Name of Jesus Christ.

I renounce every position held in the lodge by any of my ancestors, including "Tyler,""Master,""Worshipful Master," or any other. I renounce the calling of any man "Master," for Jesus Christ is my only Master and Lord, and He forbids anyone else having that title. I renounce the entrapping of others into Masonry. I renounce the effects of Masonry passed on to me and my family through any female ancestor who felt distrusted and rejected by her husband as he entered and attended any lodge and refused to tell her of his secret activities.

1ST DEGREE

I renounce the oaths taken and the curses involved in the First or Entered Apprentice degree, especially their effects on the throat and tongue. I renounce the hoodwink, the blindfold, and its effects on emotions and eyes, including all confusion, fear of the dark, fear of the light, and fear of sudden noises. I renounce the secret word, BOAZ, and all it means. I renounce the mixing and mingling of truth and error and the blasphemy of this degree of Masonry. I renounce the noose around the neck, the fear of choking, and also every spirit causing asthma, hayfever, emphysema or any other breathing difficulty. I renounce the compass point, sword or sphere held against the breast, the fear of death by stabbing pain, and the fear of heart attack from this degree.

In the Name of Jesus Christ, I now pray for healing of ___________ (throat, vocal cords, nasal passages, sinus, bronchial tubes, etc.) for healing of the speech area, and the release of the Word of God to and through me and my family.

2ND DEGREE

I renounce the oaths taken and the curses involved in the second or Fellow Craft degree of Masonry, especially the curses on the heart and chest. I renounce the secret words JACHIN and SHIBBOLETH and all that these mean. I cut off emotional hardness, apathy, indifference, unbelief, and deep anger from me and my family. In the Name of Jesus Christ, I pray for the healing of ___________ (the chest/lung/heart area) and also for the healing of my emotions and ask to be made sensitive to the Holy Spirit of God.

3RD DEGREE

I renounce the oaths taken and the curses involved in the third or Master Mason degree, especially the curses on the stomach and womb area. I renounce the secret words MAHA, BONE, MACHABEN, MACHBINNA, TUBAL CAIN, and all that they mean. I renounce the spirit of death from the blows to the head enacted as ritual murder, the fear of death, false martyrdom, fear of violent gang attack, assault, rape, and the helplessness of this degree. I renounce the falling into the coffin or stretcher involved in the ritual of murder. I renounce the false resurrection of this degree, because only Jesus Christ is the resurrection and the life! I also renounce the blasphemous kissing of the Bible on a witchcraft oath. I cut off all spirits of death, witchcraft, and deception. In the Name of Jesus Christ, I pray for the healing of ______ (the stomach, gall bladder, womb, liver, and any other organs of my body affected by masonry), and I ask for a release of compassion and understanding for me and my family.

HOLY ROYAL ARCH DEGREE

I renounce the oaths taken and the curses involved in the Holy Royal Arch Degree of Masonry, especially the oath regarding the removal of the head from the body and the exposing of the brains to the hot sun. I renounce the Mark Lodge and the mark in the form of squares and angles, which marks the person for life. I also reject the jewel or talisman which may have been made from this mark sign and worn at lodge meetings. I renounce the false, secret name of God, JAHBULON, and the password, AMMI RUHAMAH, and all they mean. I renounce the false communion or Eucharist taken in this degree and all the mockery, skepticism and unbelief about the redemptive work of Jesus Christ on the Cross of Calvary. I cut off all these curses and their effects on me and my family in the Name of Jesus Christ, and I pray for __________ (healing of the brain, the mind, etc.).

18TH DEGREE

I renounce the oaths taken and the curses involved in the eighteenth degree of Masonry, the Most Wise Sovereign Knight of the Pelican and the Eagle and Sovereign Prince Rose Croix of Heredom. I renounce and reject the Pelican witchcraft spirit as well as the occultic influence of the Rosicrucians and the Kabala in this degree. I renounce the claim that the death of Jesus Christ was a "dire calamity," and also the deliberate mockery and twisting of the Christian doctrine of the Atonement. I renounce the blasphemy and rejection of the deity of Jesus Christ and the secret words IGNE NATURA RENOVATUR INTEGRA and its burning. I renounce the mockery of the communion taken in this degree, including a biscuit, salt and white wine.

30TH DEGREE

I renounce the oaths taken and the curses involved in the thirtieth degree of Masonry, the Grand Knight Kadosh and Knight of the Black and White Eagle. I renounce the password, "STIBIU MALKABAR," and all that it means.

31ST DEGREE

I renounce the oaths taken and the curses involved in the thirty-first degree of Masonry, the Grand Inspector Inquisitor Commander. I renounce all the gods and goddesses of Egypt which are honored in this degree, including Anubis with the ram's head, Osiris the sun god, Isis the sister and wife of Osiris, and also the moon goddess. I renounce the Soul of Cheres, the false symbol of immortality, the chamber of the dead and the false teaching of reincarnation.

32ND DEGREE

I renounce the oaths taken and the curses involved in the thirty-second degree of Masonry, the Sublime Prince of the Royal Secret. I renounce Masonry's false trinitarian deity AUM and its parts; Brahma the creator, Vishnu the preserver and Shiva the destroyer. I renounce the deity of AHURA-MAZDA, the claimed or source of all light, and the worship with fire, which is an abomination to God, and the drinking from a human skull in some Rites.

YORK RITE

I renounce the oaths taken and the curses involved in the York Rite of Freemasonry, including Mark Master, Past Master, Most Excellent Master, Royal Master, Select Master, Super Excellent Master, the Orders of the Red Cross, the Knights of Malta, and the Knights Templar degrees. I renounce the secret words of JOPPA, KEB RAIOTH, and MAHER- SHALAL-HASHBAZ. I renounce the vows taken on a human skull, the crossed swords, and the curse and death wish of Judas of having the head cut off and placed on top of a church spire. I renounce the unholy communion and especially the drinking from a human skull in some rites.

SHRINERS

(America only — doesn't apply in other countries)

I renounce the oaths taken and the curses and penalties involved in the Ancient Arabic Order of the Nobles of the Mystic Shrine. I renounce the piercing of the eyeballs with a three-edged blade, the flaying of the feet, the madness, and the worship of the false god Allah as the god of our fathers. I renounce the hoodwink, the mock hanging, the mock beheading, the mock drinking of the blood of the victim, the mock dog urinating on the initiate, and the offering of urine as a commemoration.

33RD DEGREE

I renounce the oaths taken and the curses involved in the thirty-third degree of Masonry, the Grand Sovereign Inspector General. I RENOUNCE AND FORSAKE THE DECLARATION THAT LUCIFER IS GOD. I renounce the cable-tow around the neck. I renounce the death wish that the wine drunk from a human skull should turn to poison and the skeleton whose cold arms are invited if the oath of this degree is violated. I renounce the three infamous assassins of their grand master—law, property, and religion — and the greed and witchcraft involved in the attempt to manipulate and control the rest of mankind.

ALL OTHER DEGREES

I renounce all the other oaths taken, the rituals of every other degree and the curses involved. I renounce all other lodges and secret societies such as Prince Hall Freemasonry, Mormonism (which is largely based upon Masonry), The Order of Amaranth, Oddfellows, Buffalos, Druids, Foresters, Orange, Elks, Moose and Eagles Lodges, the Ku Klux Klan, The Grange, the Woodmen of the World, Riders of the Red Robe, the Knights of Pythias, the Mystic Order of the Veiled Prophets of the Enchanted Realm, the women's Orders of the Eastern Star, and the White Shrine of Jerusalem, the girls' order of the Daughters of the Eastern Star, the International Orders of Job's Daughters, the Rainbow, and the boys' Order of De Molay, and their effects on me and all my family.

I renounce the ancient pagan teaching and symbolism of the First Tracing Board, the Second Tracing Board, and the Third Tracing Board used in the ritual of the Blue Lodge. I renounce the pagan ritual of the "Point within a Circle" with all its bondages and phallus worship. I renounce the occultic mysticism of the black and white mosaic chequered floor with the tessellated border and five-pointed blazing star. I renounce the symbol "G" and its veiled pagan symbolism and bondages. I renounce and utterly forsake the Great Architect of the Universe, who is revealed in the higher degrees as Lucifer, and his false claim to be the universal fatherhood of God. I also renounce the false claim that Lucifer is the Morning Star and Shining One, and I declare that Jesus Christ is the Bright and Morning Star of Revelation 22:16.

I renounce the All-Seeing Third Eye of Freemasonry or Horus in the forehead and its pagan and occult symbolism.

I renounce all false communions taken, all mockery of the redemptive work of Jesus Christ on the Cross of Calvary, all unbelief, confusion, depression, and all worship of Lucifer as God. I renounce and forsake the lie of Freemasonry that man is not sinful, but just imperfect, and so can redeem himself through good works. I rejoice that the Bible states I am a sinner and cannot do a single thing to earn my salvation, but that I can only be saved by grace through faith in Jesus Christ and what He accomplished on the Cross of Calvary.

I renounce all fear of insanity, anguish, death wishes, suicide, and death in the Name of Jesus Christ. Death was conquered by Jesus Christ, and He alone holds the keys of death and hell, and I rejoice that He holds my life in His hands now. He came to give me life abundantly and eternally, and I believe His promises.

I renounce all anger, hatred, murderous thoughts, revenge, retaliation, spiritual apathy, false religion, all unbelief, especially unbelief in the Holy Bible as God's Word, and all compromise of God's Word. I renounce all spiritual searching into false religions and all striving to please God. I rest in the knowledge that I have found my Lord and Savior Jesus Christ and that He has found me.

I commit to burn all objects in my possession which connect me with all lodges and occultic organizations, including Masonry, witchcraft and Mormonism, and all regalia, aprons, books of rituals, rings and other jewelry. I renounce the effects that these or other objects of Masonry, such as the compass, the square, the noose or the blindfold, have had on me or my family, in Jesus' Name.

Holy Spirit, I ask that You show me anything else which I need to do or for which I should pray so that I and my family may be totally free from the consequences of the sins of Masonry, witchcraft, Mormonism, and paganism. (Pause while listening to God, and pray as the Holy Spirit leads you.) Now, dear Father God, I ask humbly for the blood of Jesus Christ, Your Son, to cleanse me from all these sins I have confessed and renounced, to cleanse my spirit, my soul, my mind, my emotions, and every part of my body which has been affected by these sins, in Jesus' Name!

I renounce every evil spirit associated with Masonry and witchcraft and all other sins, and I command in the Name of Jesus Christ for Satan and every evil spirit to be bound and to leave me now, touching or harming no one, and I send you to the feet of Jesus Himself so that He may deal with you as He sees fit. I command you never to return to me or my family. I call on the Name of the Lord Jesus to deliver me and my family of these spirits, in accordance with the many promises of the Bible. I ask to be delivered of every spirit of sickness, infirmity, curse, affliction, addiction, disease, or allergy associated with these sins which I have confessed and renounced.

I surrender to God's Holy Spirit and to no other spirit all the places in my life where these sins have been. I ask You, Lord, to baptize me in Your Holy Spirit now according to the promises in Your Word. I take to myself the whole armor of God in accordance with Ephesians chapter six and rejoice in its protection as Jesus surrounds me and fills me with His Holy Spirit. I enthrone You, Lord Jesus, in my heart, for You are my Lord and my Savior, the source of eternal life. Thank

You, Father God, for Your mercy, Your forgiveness, and Your love. In the Name of Jesus Christ, Amen.

*These Freemasonry prayers are taken from Unmasking Freemasonry - Removing the Hoodwink by Selwyn Stevens, Jubilee Publishers, PO Box 36-044, Wellington 6330, New Zealand. (ISBN 0 9583417-3-7). Copying of these prayers is both permitted and encouraged, provided reference is made to their origination, as noted here. Freemasonry prayers from The Unmasking of Freemasonry by Selwyn Stevens, available from Dove Ministries, PO Box 48036 Blockhouse Bay, Auckland, New Zealand.

www.ingramcontent.com/pod-product-compliance
Lightning Source LLC
Chambersburg PA
CBHW081331120626
46546CB00011B/3298
9781954509108